PITH & WRY

_for Heather —
also on the writing
path —_

[signature]

Keep writing !

Roger N...

Special thanks to Roger Nash, Consulting Editor

PITH & WRY

CANADIAN POETRY

EDITED BY
SUSAN MCMASTER

ScrivenerPress

Library and Archives Canada Cataloguing in Publication

Pith & wry : Canadian poetry / Susan McMaster, editor.

Includes index.
Some poems previously published in SugarMule.com #33.
ISBN 978-1-896350-41-7

1. Canadian poetry (English)—21st century. I. McMaster, Susan, 1950- II. Title: Pith & wry.

PS8273.P58 2010   C811'.6080971   C2010-904809-1

CONSULTING EDITOR: Roger Nash
ARTWORK AND BOOK DESIGN: Gwen Frankton
Front and back covers: *Hawthorne,* mixed media on Yupo paper
Entry Points (p. 13): *Pine,* pen and ink
Beware (p. 27): *Hawthorne in Flower,* pen and ink
The Story Tellers (p. 53): *Nest,* pen and ink
Appetite (p. 85): *High-bush Cranberry,* pen and ink
Pith & Wry (p. 109): *Buckthorne,* pen and ink
A-New (p. 133): *Honeysuckle in Spring,* pen and ink

Published by Scrivener Press
465 Loach's Road,
Sudbury, Ontario, Canada, P3E 2R2
info@yourscrivenerpress.com
www.scrivenerpress.com

We acknowledge the support of the Canada Council for the Arts and the Ontario Arts Council for our publishing program.

ONTARIO ARTS COUNCIL
CONSEIL DES ARTS DE L'ONTARIO

Canada Council   Conseil des Arts
for the Arts   du Canada

PREFACE

Canada abounds with poets. Today, our poetry is read and honoured at home and around the globe. This is not accidental. Our trademark mix of an open political environment; generous government support; public lending rights and copyright protection; a national, publicly funded broadcasting corporation and a culturally savvy media; a network of literary publishers, publications, readings, and festivals; prestigious, richly endowed prizes; Can-lit, and writing programs at all levels; and, most important, readers who love poetry and buy books—all combine to produce a society in which poets thrive.

Not only thrive, but multiply. The poetry community now embraces several thousand practitioners in all styles and delivery methods, from the most traditional to the most experimental. Hundreds of poetry books and publications every year join an equal number of performance and digital presentations to draw standing room only audiences and win international awards.

After almost three decades of writing and editing poetry in Canada, I know a number of fine poets from across the land, many represented in *Pith & Wry*. Not all appear here, of course: it's clearly impossible to include all the excellent Canadian writers in any anthology. So I have taken the time-honoured course of simply presenting some of the poets whose work I like and admire, poets who have been my peers, my companions, my critics, and my mentors throughout my writing life. The collection of poems thus gathered is not authoritative, it does not cover every region and voice and official language, it sidesteps performance and digital material better presented in other forms. What it does include is outstanding work by poets who have won international renown for their contributions to world literature. It presents a substantial selection from nationally known poets in their prime. And it includes contributions from poets who speak with fresh voices at the edge of innovation.

Virtually all the poems in *Pith & Wry* are new, written by living, working authors. The anthology offers a wide range of styles and voices, from the subtle obliques of minimalist forms, through the direct intensities of contemporary lyricism, post-modernist narrative, and "people's poetry," to the vigorous offspring of L=A=N=G=U=A=G=E poetry and deconstruction. Pre-millennial pieces by two of our major writers (including a previously uncollected poem: see Notes) are a gift for literary historians and an insight into a time of ferment. The contributors to this volume are similarly widespread in a geographical sense, hailing from Victoria to St. John's, from Iqaluit to Windsor.

Above all, this anthology presents poems and poets that twinge my sense of the strange, the beyond. Poems that cut straight to the pith—while at the same time casting a wry eye of mature understanding on human passions and despairs. Poets who've written something I'd never imagined, and now can't forget.

While assembling *Pith & Wry*, I came across the *Anthology of Canadian Poetry (English)*, edited by Ralph Gustafson for Pelican Books in 1942. He opened his introduction with the traditional apologia—"Some readers will find many omissions in this anthology"—and continued with words that might serve as my own almost seventy years later:

> In my task as compiler…I have measured and judged my material not by historical significance nor by "Canadianism," but in terms of vitality: is it alive or dead? If it deepened experience, caught at the heart and mind with poetic power—and was technically concentric—it was for this book.

And for this book. Maybe some of what follows will catch you, too, by the pith, by the wry—and stay.

—*Susan McMaster, Ottawa, July 2010*

ACKNOWLEDGEMENTS

The majority of poems in *Pith & Wry: Canadian Poetry* were first collected at the request of M. L. (Marc) Weber, editor of the literary magazine *Sugar Mule*, an e-zine from the United States, for a Canadian issue which he asked me to compile as guest editor. This is possibly the first time an American magazine editor has reached across the border to fill his publication from first page to last with Canadian poetry, and I thank him again for the opportunity. *Sugar Mule: The Canadian Issue* appeared in November 2009 (#33). It was warmly received, and Marc suggested publishing it as an anthology.

The generous offer by poet Roger Nash to act as consulting editor was decisive in convincing me to go ahead. Roger showed the manuscript to Laurence Steven, publisher of Scrivener Press, who immediately agreed to take it on. Friend and artist Gwen Frankton, who also illustrated *Sugar Mule* #33, offered to do the book design, including creating six new art works. Marc gave his permission for use of the *Sugar Mule* files. The 35 original poets were enthusiastic, as were the 10 additional writers I invited to participate—most known to me but including a few new discoveries suggested by Roger and Laurence. Thanks are also due to Yvonne Earle, Legislative Librarian at the Legislative Assembly of Nunavut, for helping me contact Laakkuluk Williamson Bathory, and to Gwen, for making me aware of Laakkuluk's work.

To all who have made *Pith & Wry* a reality, I am deeply grateful: to Roger and Gwen and Laurence, without whose hard work, practical support, and intelligent advice this volume would never have appeared; to the poets across the country who have so generously trusted their work to my hands; and of course to my husband, Ian, and my family and friends, who have once again offered wholehearted support.

—*SM*

CONTENTS

PITH & WRY 109

A-NEW 133

ENTRY POINTS

DAVE MARGOSHES

Saskatchewan poet and fiction writer Dave Margoshes has published widely in literary magazines and anthologies. *Bix's Trumpet and Other Stories* was named Book of the Year at the 2007 Saskatchewan Book Awards. Some of the following poems appear in his new book, *Dimensions of an Orchard* (Black Moss, 2010), reprinted by permission of the author.

High wire act

See this high wire, this tight rope?
They string it between then and now, grease
it good, dare you
to step out, shred the net, set up
wind machines, start the lions roaring, spread
shattered glass below, and that's all just
for openers. Then they tell ya stay home,
you got nuthin' to prove.

Worm's eye view

A world, spinning through clouds
insubstantial as your breath
on a morning in January.
On the world, puddles of cobalt, islands
of emerald, cinnamon, ivory.
On this island, hills, mountains,
forests, plains, meadows.
At the edge of this meadow, a tree,
American elm, gritting its teeth
against the remorseless stare
of the beetle, its arms raised
in resignation. In the crook
of one branch, a nest, a whorl
of grass, earth, twigs, a frightwig.
In this tangle, a bird, its breast
raging, its eye vivid. In the beak
of the bird, a worm, more resigned
than even the tree. In the eye
of the worm, a world, spinning
through insubstantial cloud.

Armstrong's foot

Blake's fearsome tyger
stuffed and raffled off
on the midway, Jonah's whale
a cartoon pitch
for tuna, the snake
in the garden just a torn strip
of inner tube after all, the moon
when Armstrong's foot left
its mark nothing more
than the green cheese
my grannie always said
it would be, cheese
filled with holes.

In love with decay

I stood in line at the Safeway, my basket laden
with rotting fruit. There were cherries glutinous
in their sugared blood, blueberries marbled
with sepulchral mould, molten strawberries
laced with slime and fragrant as sulfur, peaches
and plums all softboiled eggs, all puppy belly.

A woman in a flowered dress and cheeks rosy
as a newborn's turned away, holding
her nose, but the checkout clerk looked through
me, saw that I was in love with decay, with the rapture
of destruction. Gently, she placed my purchases
in a paper bag she drew from under the till,
jewels too precious for plastic. Then I set off
home, drunk with the possibilities of life.

What was it Eliot said?

The hair in my nostrils grows white. My penis
stretches, yawns, rolls over into its pillow, desire
courses through me like flickering light
in a storm. A mosquito bows its head at the well
of my pale blood and hesitates. My joints
sing, *a cappella*, my empty palms ache. Outside
the window, sparrows congregate at the feeder
like old women on the stoops of Brooklyn
when I was a boy, noisy and vivid in their scarves,
their arms filled with the absence of their
children, lost in the war or to illnesses
now mercifully extinct. These birds regard me
as the women might, with neither contempt
nor indifference, they know I feed them, asking
nothing in return, and their gratitude pulses
in the blue sheen of their throats, but remains
unspoken. When I open the door, they explode
like gravel sprayed from the tires of a speeding car.
Their song thrums in the absence their shape
carves into the fragrant air, a reproach,
a warning.

DON MCKAY

Don McKay has written many books of poetry and two of wilderness poetics. Several of these have been recognized with awards—the Governor General's Award and Griffin Poetry Prize among them. He has lived all over Canada and currently resides in St. John's, Newfoundland.

Slow Spring on Vancouver Island

In the understory, *sotto voce*,
crypto-birds rehearse. Is
that you, Junco
setting your Hopkins-self aside
to sip-sip-sip so
generically? That you, Varied thrush,
clearing your throat *ad
nauseam*, uncertain
as the rain which quits, dithers,
threatens, finally
compromises on the drizzle into which
your indecipherable ciphers fit like inter-
office memoranda?
                            Over the dun
duff of the forest floor one alder leaf—
thinned by winter to its skeleton—
hangs like a glyph.
Foliose lichens urge their hypergreens.
One day soon—
so goes the tale—Junco's voice
will quicken into trill, its quick lusts
gargling. Varied thrush will thrust its whistle-hum
frankly into the mix, and that last leaf—
like an icon suddenly
relaxing to cliché—
uncling. And then—by
the Jesus we'll be on our way.

Crinoid

A fossil, preposterous
and common, light
as a dime, as infinity's
poker chip, a small grey
Tylenol-sized disk you can
slip into your pocket
or cup in your palm.
Turn it on end,
you can see where a delicate fishline
ran down its core. Reel it in,
you'll haul up Ordovician oceans
where they boogied and grew, vertebrae
with frond-like arms and bloom-like heads
asway in the tide that fed them, as the mind
of Wang Wei in the ever-adjusting
wind.
        O Chordates, you'll exclaim
to our distinguished many-membered phylum,
spare a moment to applaud
this alien far off flowering spine.
                        O Elvis,
wherever you are,   .
shake it with the snakes that first
shook it.

KATIA GRUBISIC

Montreal poet Katia Grubisic is a writer, editor, and translator whose work has been published in Canada and internationally. Her book *What if red ran out* (Goose Lane) was short-listed for the A. M. Klein Prize for Poetry and won the 2009 Gerald Lampert Memorial Award for best first book of poetry in Canada.

Landing

In the form of a carcass, what used to be a canoe waits
in the underbrush. Ours is not to deliver it from itself.

We have landed here after what seemed great
struggle against the current but now that we're pulled up

it's the kind of place guardian angels are buried
alive, where people go mad from lead poisoning

or sorrow.—The light leans
into the clearing in the wrong shape,

its patterns not its own. Nowhere is properly barren,
doesn't work that way. Don't flatter yourself

into thinking that you'll have been longed for,
awaited. We've been heading north, true or other.

The shield up here is green, artefacts pose
for photographs—axe handle, ruby necklace—

the shaved-animal mountain would cover itself with its hands
if it could. We always seek a more sepia way to say it.

Here is what they've done and there, a girl lived
on a hillside for a summer, sleeping under a railroad

trestle. It's the frame that concerns us,
all that's left the pine thwarts, some rope, the gunwales and keel

worried through. Shall we go further,
to where the islands begin to extricate themselves

from the horizon? Won't you make me a lifetime of Persian carpets
of cedar and pine? Each year a different shade of green, lighter, to orange

until they're ready, right flammable. If I stayed here long enough
would I receive weatherstained postcards from myself,

of granite blown raw along the road or its bulbous grey
knuckling a lake. The words blurred

into you-are-heres, morose ink insects leaving us
divinations we don't care to interpret. Would I join those nocturnes

from the wolves, that wafting confirmation.
If I drew them now they would be death

leaning far over. I try to make up my mind
to stay—it would look like this,

the mad colours of the gneiss become still
life, covered in the silks of rain upon rain upon rain.

PENN KEMP

Poet Penn Kemp, from London, Ontario, performs in arts festivals worldwide, expanding boundaries with 25 books of poetry and drama, 10 recordings of "Sound Opera" and sound poetry, Canada's first poetry CD-ROM, and 6 award-winning videopoems. The League of Canadian Poets has proclaimed her a foremother of Canadian poetry.

Crowning

Lying here on a white bed
I'm covered by a blue towel
in a white room in Tulum.

Through the open arch is
the bath of blue and white
tile whose pattern I have
studied in photo on photo.

Here two dimensions spring
to three, to four, as time coll-
apses. I attend my daughter

in spirit nine months ago as
she perched on the birthing
stool, in that blue tiled bath
pushing a small head through.

Through the long dawn
irate jackdaws pierce a sound poem
to roosters. Dogs and men return

to their own labour with the slap of
shovels. Calls cross species tell all.
Telling. Here we are. Here. Now

nine-month-old Ula stands across
from her mamesi, braced almost
steady in her playpen, and beams.

We circle our bellies in the old
way, simulating birth, calling down
ancestor women, whirling alongside

the great grandmothers who recede
in the space of a year and re-appear

as we sweep in their wake among
the black-braided women of Tulum,
ocean rhythm, blue sky on white sand.

Truly croned, crowned grandmother,
I circle the long line of women: daughter
-to-daughter-to-daughter. Drawn again

by the weight of love into the spiral dance.

Recurring Dream Doctrine

Night rustles outside our window, murmurs
and squeaks. Whimpers follow outraged
raccoon yowl. Orange and black streak

across the dark pane I can't see through
into night creatures' world, conjuring
interlaced smells of skunk, mouse, bat

disturbing our neighbour hound's nose.
Scent leads a trail to territorial war, deep
enmities nurtured throughout the long

hours before dawn lifts that velvet cloth to
reveal grey, seeping shade back to clarity.
Daylight cicada notions begin threading a

brightening air. Dragonflies wing-web
the pond. Inside I still dream of prowling
tiger. Similars, signature. Like calls to like

out of time. Speaking harmonies. Chords
lift. Given so much, we reach for more
even when full. Over.

KATE EICHHORN

Kate Eichhorn is the author of *Fond* (BookThug, 2008), which was short-listed for the Gerald Lampert Memorial Award, and co-editor of *Prismatic Publics: Innovative Canadian Women's Poetry and Poetics* (Coach House, 2009). She teaches Cultural Studies at The New School, New York. This selection is from her forthcoming collection from BookThug.

from Fieldnotes, a forensic

One perfect autumn day I attended 11 funerals
people lined the street awaiting loved ones with open graves
I stood behind a middle-aged man

"If you cared, you wouldn't carry a thin blade
between villages," a pseudonymic photograph of my dead
who touched me on the shoulder

wished I could give him 1000 marks
some answers

Most people spilled with foreignness
this weekly harvest of respects provided closure
I was filled with the bounty of a completed job

"How did he die?"

looked at my clipboard and answered,
"There were landmines in the nature of the injuries"

I craft these freshly dug statements to investigate
our consumption of fear
contemplate academics repatriating the impossibility of war
to console ourselves with bodies in coffins

I drove from village to village with my ethnic-cleansing methodology
several flatly told me they had had extensive contact
with soldiers in sneakers

the purpose of this text was dutifully transcribed
with incomprehensible terror

An onlooker tells me in a language I do not speak
"You do not see because you have units of analysis
such as states"

For those who had given us permission, obligation boiled to write
for the exhumed but decomposition has never been
a picturesque rural village under thunder

This is a bodily observation
the most radical of all ideas

Not far from where we were indiscriminate in a sunlit clearing
the world unfolds

always inscribed on my knowledge-producing warfare
an obligation to other bodies, demanding colleagues

personification into units behind artillery
result of perfect planning

BEWARE

LORNA CROZIER

Lorna Crozier is a winner of the Governor General's Award for Poetry for *Inventing the Hawk*. She has published fifteen books of poetry, and has just had a memoir, *Small Beneath the Sky*, published by Greystone Books. She teaches at the University of Victoria and lives outside the city with poet Patrick Lane.

Angel of Loneliness

Of course there's no one,
especially not an angel
though the air seems overly receptive
as if it's leaving room for something
to arrive. The only tracks in the snow
are her own, leading from the back door
to the birdfeeder where wind above the drifts
fashions wings of such a force and size
she can feel the muscles
underneath the pinions as they push her back
and sweep across the yard.

There's no one here but her,
a lone woman breaking
a path to the feeder, her body
all these years untouched,
unfeathered. It's the cold—
this winter there's too much of it—
that makes its presence known,
inside and out. She can feel it
blunt her skin, grip the morning
and all that's tethered to the earth
in its unforgiving fist.

Angel of Grief

He shows up in my mother's bedroom,
wings soiled, all down the sides
piss-yellow stains, the rust of blood,
and along the feathers' hem a dazzling green
as if, to get to me, he flew too low across the sea
and gathered up its phosphorescence.

Part of me understands why he is here—
I've grief enough and there's something
sacred about this place and what I'm doing,
emptying my mother's dresser,
the only thing she claimed as hers alone,
the house too small, too poor to keep a secret.

She warned me as a child not to snoop
but I find nothing in the drawers a daughter
shouldn't see: two old swimsuits, hand-made,
loosening around the legs, white cotton bras
and briefs she ordered from the catalogue,
a few with bare elastic showing, all intimate
and washed and washed—I couldn't be sadder.

The angel doesn't speak, at least not here,
not to me, but there's a susurration
in the room as if he's brought the wind with him
to keep alive his wings. He won't be trapped.
I've yet to see his face. I don't know if
he is weeping. His head is bowed, white
hair falling over ears and forehead
—enough of him. Here, he's less
important than my mother, her last things;
they slip through my fingers to the garbage sack
and leave their mark on me like scalding water.

Extreme Creation

The hummingbird—small,
fierce flower, its long stamen
hardened to a beak stitching the air
as if its purpose was to needlepoint
a sampler of summer's beauty.

God cut it from its stem,
fastened tiny feet
and let it fly. This happened
on the last day in the hour
set aside so he could look
at what he'd done, do a double-take,

turn blossoms into birds and visa versa,
dapple, split, ravish, shim
into the million things he'd made
the outrageous (deepening the dip
behind the human collarbone, painting
red stripes on the long cheeks of the turtle)

outrageous beauty and its opposite:

the shit-brown
slime of wood slugs
to which he added, to mix it up,
more delicate than newborn fingers,
two soft horns
touched with the tip of his tongue
to make them shine.

The Ambiguity of Clouds

Never mind, the clouds say
as they drift above her. Never mind.
When you first heard them
as a child, you thought they meant

let it go, don't fuss about it,
believing the phrase implied
all would be fine
if you didn't obsess, if you didn't
let things fester.

Time has taught you another
meaning; death has taught you,
loneliness has taught you.
It's never the mind
that gets you close to beauty,
the first and last of things,
or any of the wisdoms you long to know.
There's no word for what can take you there

though it has something to do with the eyes of horses,
the body's workings, whiskers sandpapering across a cheek,
a woman's laugh loud enough to bend a row
of ripening wheat. Who laughed
like that and when? And where were you?

Never mind, never mind,
is it possible the clouds say that,
mindless as they are? All
body, if you can call them that,
cumulative and shifting shape,

mare's tails, ephemera, fish bones,
a lung bleached of blood,
an inky brain, not thinking,
just folding and refolding all afternoon
long sheets of rain. They never mind.

Finally

The word Love means someone takes you
in your old clothes, your face too bare, too open,
when someone fastens the buttons on your coat
as if you've fallen back through sixty years to be
a child again, when someone takes you onto the path
holding you by the arm, your feet not knowing what
they used to know, your feet in rubber boots stumbling,
blind to roots and stones, when someone takes you
to the ocean, the water also in the air raining down
its saltless weeping, the word Love means someone
takes you to the rocks, rain too heavy for the gulls
to fly, three bobbing like windless boats, all sails
and heartbeat, Love leaves you there, no words
for it now, you and the gulls and the ocean
that moves as far away from you as it can go.

MARY ANN MULHERN

Mary Ann Mulhern's first three books address leaving the convent; being an undertaker's daughter (Acorn-Plantos People's Poetry Award shortlist); and sexual abuse by priests in Windsor, Ontario, her hometown. "magic charm" and "petition of mary easty" are from *Sleeping with Satan: Salem Witch-hunt, 1692* (Black Moss Press, 2010); reprinted by permission of the author.

magic charm

in the courtroom
a witness says
I've sewn
a magic charm
beneath the skin
of my left arm
the Devil's gift
the judge clutches
a leather pouch
worn around his neck
herbs preserved with wax
to ward off spells
cast from the shine
of hair and eyes and lips
I smell his potion
crushed hawthorn leaves
and fruit
rich-red and green
taken from the tree
that offers branches
high and wide and strong
enough for the swing
of a wealthy witch
her prison gown
blown into a blossom
tossed over a grave

petition of mary easty

my hand reaches for a pen
paper white as death
waiting for my words
testament of innocence
my accusers shape lies
into steps of a courtroom dance
spells of the two-faced moon
young girls chant names
of withered witches
hanged from a Salem rope
knots threaded with thorns

I plead for release
from the shame of this cell
stain of my prison dress
the judge folds my plea
into a lonely scaffold
where I can barely stand
blots of ink blind the sun
every star in a Godless sky

the executioner

I watch him
loose black tunic
bright cross
large on his chest

he looks up at me
silent chained afraid
just another witch
this man has no fear
of an evil eye
he is the one
who holds magic
who strikes fire from flint

his mind is a flame
that flashes over me
radiant as Satan's smile

released

after a year
of the rack, the black pit
red-hot irons
scraps of bread
i am released
hair scissored short
eyes silent grey
my body a shadow
risen from the grave
a witch who passes close
on the village road
silver rosary
tarnished black
in the crooked
gnarl of hands
tight knot of veins
every bead a curse

HEATHER SPEARS

Heather Spears has published 11 collections of poetry, 4 novels, 3 books of drawings, and a book on visual perception. Honours include the Bronfman, Lowther, and Governor General's awards. She was educated in British Columbia and Copenhagen, where she has lived since 1962, and travels widely in Canada, the Middle East, Europe, and America. (www.heatherspears.com)

Obscurant

White phosphorous
like a net
in the night sky
cast with exquisite precision
great dolorous spines, outlines
of a skirt a mile wide, a dome, an embrace
soft extensions of descending woolly light
choreographed, unhurried

Beautiful
you have to say it
you are not even at the border
like the journalist telling about it or the other one
who is filming it
as it happens LIVE printed across the screen
you are far away in Europe they can't see
what will happen either, what is beginning
now to happen
as the obscurant
so meticulously measured
begins to touch and touch the ground between the buildings
doing what it does best,
predicted

14 Jan. 09

A sent photo

A child's face
plane with the pavement
like a mosaic
pieced, flat
the pavement is a house levelled
the word is rubble
the word is collateral
a child's face
flat to the ground
gray, inset
a perfect fit
the earth and bricks and bits of cement
pressed around it
no blood
not even her hair
just the entire face
moon round
part of the picture
icon among all the other fragments
melted into one surface
so tight
not even her shoulders

You saw it before you could stop seeing it
stop seeing it, you will
never stop seeing it
just her face
eyes closed
they have to be, or the sky overhead
could no longer bear

14 Jan. 09

JAN CONN

Jan Conn's recent book is *Botero's Beautiful Horses* (Brick, 2009). Her work is widely published, for example in *The Best Canadian Poetry in English Anthology* (Tightrope, 2009). Prizes include the 2006 *Malahat Review* P. K. Page Founders' Award and a 2003 CBC Literary Award. She lives in Great Barrington, Massachusetts. (www.janconn.com)

Background of Enchantments

Matchstick stairs lead to a dollhouse kitchen,
twig bridge from one box to the next,
roofs with near-perfect pitch
slumped in exhaustion, a bust of a man

in jaunty sailor hat digresses frantically from prepared speech,
chimneys bob up and down
like player piano keys, a Russian farmer steps out of Tolstoy
    and finds the mildewed, wood-framed church

aslant, his hat and potatoes sunk in mud, a parachutist
behind enemy lines years out of date.

•

Night the wide unblinking eye of a chameleon,
we're afloat in the unconscious,
motor cavalcade and Jackie in a lamé suit, destined for
a handshake or a goodnight kiss, my appetite, your mouth.

Love is now a view of an interior in flames, a metal jacket,
in lieu of touch there's an earthquake,
we're pitched forward on hands and knees, coming to rest
    face to face with a depot of used tires, a parking lot.

The Character of the Accidental

Light beaming from the roses at dangerously delinquent
velocities makes a pact with the subliminally erotic.
                    Why don't you?

Blurry circles, AKA soap bubbles in
infrared time, are strewn across the seascape,
so provocatively and distractingly we suspect
they are harbingers of bizarre, conical cloud formations.

In one of her introspective moods she wears
cherries hooked over her ears.
Her irascible pet iguana, sunning head-first
between her breasts,
scares off prospective beaux.

Unexpectedly the cold swells and billows over us—
it's how we recognize it, the way forward,
negotiate with ice crystals
and hope the violent wind
doesn't whirl the unmoored house off to Uranus.

Arrival of the Nightingale

The pavilion by starlight is dim, unexpected,

Klee changes the viewpoint to an atmosphere
on the edge of a tropical storm.

Red slices of moons, blood oranges.

The exposition is complicated by the arrival of the nightingale.
The Middle Ages are not heaven-sent

but arrive fourth-class, behind the engine,
covered in soot and grime.

Despite migraine the nightingale attempts to please
the burgeoning, erratic winds,
lurid in crepuscular light.

Easy to believe visible reality is merely one isolated phenomenon
among many,
the drops now falling faster and harder.

I know in the desert we'd live for such rain,
and the ensuing rainflowers passionately bursting into bloom.

Here, we walk hand-in-hand, the down-at-the-heels road
about to lead us astray

like a bus ride across the continent, and we're inside the storm
sitting wide-awake, passing circular trees, some

sliced neatly in two as though a madman had visited
with plumb-line and saw.

The bus veers west, then the storm passes
trailing an exhaust of murky sky.

Night seems endless, the road follows
fallen stars back and forth across a plain

—birdsong becomes birdbones, lost melody.

Maureen Scott Harris

Maureen Scott Harris was born in Prince Rupert, grew up in Winnipeg, and lives in Toronto. Awards include the Trillium Book Award for Poetry for *Drowning Lessons* (2005), the *Prairie Fire* creative non-fiction prize (2007), and the WildCare Tasmania Nature Writing Prize (2009).

Fragmentary Life

Nightly I rise up through water, then submerge again, over and over, swimming or drifting through dream after dream, liquid and changeable. Like eel or seal, I undulate from surface to depth and back, in and out of light and dark, through a moil of other creatures. Some inarticulate preoccupation the dark urgent current on which we ride.

Waking I shed dreams
like water, only a drop
clings
here and there
refracting light.

Listing

Bubble bath, she thinks, bubble bath.
And calcium. A bar of good chocolate.
There was something else—I'm sure
there was something else. She bends
again to the keyboard, its intricate
possibilities. And or but? Which or that?
The alphabet remains impassive, waiting
for her to choose. But how?
So much on offer—uncountable
combinations of 26. Dizzying. The list
in her head starts to fade. Bubble bath,
she repeats—b—b—b—all those b's
round bubbles themselves with tails
flung to the sky. She herself is more
like a g—that g from good perhaps,
a bubble dragged down to the ground,
subdued, still.

Something to Say

This *thing* that I wanted to tell you, this—
this—motion. The way I moved through the city
which was also moving, and the two motions
together made a drift, continual and giddy.
Some days, remembering,
the view is washed with water as if seen
through the sheer of a cascade.

But today it's snow drifting down, coasting, silencing
all but the indoor hums, the murmurs
of fridge and washing machine, water running (even here,
water) through the pipes of the radiator. And along
Yonge Street the crowd washes into and out of
stores and banks, alleyways, streetcars,
averted from the one who sits on the sidewalk wrapped
in a blanket, head bowed, and that other
flung on the heating grate, limp.

It lurks out there. That also is what I wanted
to tell you, the city circling and circling out until it drains
into the lake and floods across the countryside.
Bleak now in the damp snow falling while I sit motionless.
And this thing, this motion I thought to show you,
tell you, is for the moment only
a smear across the view obstructing and obstructing
like the sheep dog that turns the sheep
in a slow curve out towards the stony pasture, their little hoofed
feet lifting and descending on the rocky path, slippery
in the aftermath of deep snow, a stutter
like this this   this   *thing*

Sunday Morning, November

outside the window
green cedar, fading ginkgo
shake under rain

only half-awake
I stare at the opaque sky—
crack! crash!

yellow-leafed maple
baring itself—naked
rain-blackened branches

tremble of lightning
red leaves flare on the street
then dull

even the squirrels
flatten in the jagged light
houses hunker down

Heather Ferguson

Heather Ferguson, an editor and translator from Ottawa, is the author of *The Lapidary* (Vermillon, 2009). Her work has appeared in the anthologies *Symbiosis* and *Sounds New*, and in such publications as *Alter Vox*, *Anthos*, *Arc*, and *Ygdrusil*.

Visiting my mother

I kneel
to help my father
with his shoes

    he boards the bus
    unsteadily
    we sit at the front

        he leans sideways
        to look discreetly
        at a toddler

            my bag splits
            treats for my mother
            roll across the bus

                strong gusts buffet us
                on the short walk
                to the home

                    flowers and chairs
                    a welcoming patio
                    mask the locked door

        how time jumps around
        my mother says
        amused

    a senior grabs me
    lovingly—*oh mother,*
    I've missed you so much!

    by the fence
    my parents talk
    alone in the yard

my mother gives
the paring knife
an odd look

    she wears her new ring
    with the fake diamond
    turned in

        picnic supper
        we watch the ants
        and say little

            a senior sits
            slumped in her wheelchair, her chin
            on her teddy bear

                there on the toilet
                a resident, absorbed
                and in plain view

                    he raped her right there
                    to force her to talk
                    my mother says

                June heat
                she speaks of her part—Mary—
                in a Christmas play

        my father
        listens intently
        ignores his coffee

    summer afternoon
    my mother prepares
    for bed

back home, my father
absent-mindedly pours himself
a glass of vinegar

SYLVIA ADAMS

Ottawa writer Sylvia Adams is the author of the poetry collections *Mondrian's Elephant* (Cranberry Tree Poetry Chapbook Contest national winner) and *Sleeping on the Moon* (2007 runner-up Lampman-Scott Poetry Award), the novel *This Weather of Hangmen*, and a children's book in verse, *Dinner at the Dog Pound*. (www.sylviaadamspublications)

Listening for the Dead

1

My father's death surprised him
as much as anyone.
A stroke they said, like his mother before him.
No warning except for an aching neck
the day before. He didn't know what a headache was,
said my mother, who'd suffered from migraines
all her life. He was preparing
for bed one night, thinking perhaps
of Hallowe'en candy, in case the grandchildren came.
Or planning, at last, a Florida winter.
My mother heard him fall.

By the time I drove across town to the old stuccoed house,
there was my father, who'd vowed to leave this world
a tidy place, debt-free, being carried out
in a blanket, a doctor as old as himself
struggling to keep those cold, pale feet
from bumping the stairs.
Don't look, someone said. Or perhaps
I imagined they said it.
Toward morning, we tried to sleep—
I on the couch in the living room,
my disbelieving mother, and my grandmother,
who lived with them and needed us both
to help her up the stairs.
I kept listening for him
but the shadows were shocked into silence.

II

The winter after he died, his slippers whispered
across the carpet, the way they did
when, at four, I lay on my stomach, shading
Rapunzel's hair with my favourite jumbo pink crayon.
He stood at the kitchen phone,
receiver to ear in voiceless dialogue.
Perhaps in repeating daily rituals
he would discover that nothing had changed.

Early the following May, I dreamed that he sat
at a banquet table, eating cake with strangers.
I called to him, but he rose
and walked away into dazzling air.
Wait! Take me with you! I called.
He turned and held out his hand: Not yet—
the light an ovation of white beyond him.
I woke, his hand still nudging mine.
Why hadn't I said, Come back?

III

My mother takes flowers to the cemetery
in containers she knows won't get stolen.
Is she thinking
how the lilacs she brings brush her cheek
like fingertips of the dead,
how my grandmother's mouth opens like a bird's,
waiting for ice cream?

SUSAN MCMASTER

Ottawa poet Susan McMaster has published 16 books and recordings, and edited some 40 anthologies, catalogues, and magazines. This series from *Crossing Arcs: Alzheimer's, My Mother, and Me* (Black Moss, 2009/10) includes comments in italics made by her mother, Betty Page, in response to the poems. (http://web.ncf.ca/smcmaster)

I am lost, Mother
in the spaces you leave behind

I cannot even see
    a shadow there to
        follow

             I have no way to comfort you in the
             empty room
             your mind now is

                  doors and windows
                  shut

                  blinds hung
                  closed

I don't think I have Alzheimer's. My memory is my own and I'm going to keep it!

If this happens to me
I will kill myself.
I don't mean to let the words out.
And with my daughters,
manage to refrain.
But to him, they slip out suddenly
through cracks in conversation,
at stopped moments in halls.
Nights, I plan the method
that will cause least pain.
Look most like an accident.
Google has thousands of recipes
but none is certain.

Not Scotch and pills at midnight:
they say you vomit it up.
Not slipping through a hole in ice:
someone is always watching.
And which house, which lake
will I choose to forever poison
for those left behind?
There will be no more words.
Not even, I'm not sorry.

I had to get angry. There's anger and fear, one or the other,
and I chose anger. Anger is what keeps you alive.

She takes off her boots.
Coat still buttoned,
turns from the hall
into the apartment
she left a week before.
One final trip to pick up
final things.

Steps through the arch
into the living room.

Her hands come together.
Fold around each other
as if against cold.
The couch is gone.
Her lamp.
Her chair.
The floor a mess
of movers' tracks.

A few more steps.
She stops.
Bends her head
into my shoulder.
I put my arms around her—

her hands, between us,
closed around something
no-one can hold.

Acceptance and loss. Holding on to life and what it was.

What does it mean?
Is it just a bad joke?
I hold all that's happened
up to my eyes
as if it were jumbled
in a child's kaleidoscope,
turn the tube through tumbles
of yellow, red, blue—
shards and slivers and fragments
in a cracked cascade
that clink into place
after place
after place
with a small glass hiss.
Why her? Why this?
I turn and turn.
Each burst is different.
Each unrelated to the one before.

*This is not reality, my reality. This is where you go when you're
finished.*

And yet, she's still here.
Still behind the windows
lit by gas lamps and firelight,
still leading the beat
in family songs,
still at the centre,
with her laugh-tooled skin
and quartz-blue eyes
and hair like a silver mop,

still here, as she burnishes
from grey to glow—

    and her words fly away like
    flickers, gulls
    tossing in wind—

        memories spray and tangle like
        ribbons of mist
        steaming from the bay—

            thoughts come and go like
            flames in the stove, like
            the wiver of a candle, like

                the breath that blows back
                into the crowded room

      as I slip away
      into salt and damp,
      into darkness by the shore.

    Look back through the glass.

Look back
as my mother,
small and gold,
slips into my hands

    and I close my palms
    around her,
        hold her
            as the current
                rushes her down.

THE
STORY
TELLERS

MARTY GERVAIS

Marty Gervais has published a dozen poetry books, plus plays, essays, and a novel, winning the Acorn-Plantos and Harbourfront Festival prizes. He is a columnist at the *Windsor Star*; the Resident Writing Professional, University of Windsor; managing editor, *Windsor Review*; and founder of Black Moss Press. These poems appear in *Lucky Days* (Mosaic, 2009).

Imagining Myself Bearing Good News

At dawn, the corridors are silent
and I wander the hospital
I get off at the second floor
see the north wing entrance
draped with Do Not Enter tape
the nursing station abandoned
metal racks now empty of
patients' binders
the wing shut down
lights dimmed
I am walking at the bottom of the sea
imagine the drift and heave
of plant life, pyramids of form
eerie fish drifting in slow motion
in this muted ballet of form and ritual
The doors to rooms are opened
wide like forlorn outstretched hands
of the souls of Purgatory or barn
doors left swinging in a storm or
doors of a wrecked ship lodged
in the havoc of sand
I am walking at the bottom of the sea
alone and silent among the dead
a place of faint memories
extinct clangour of rolling carts
breakfast trays and footsteps
amid hushed prayers of the ill
I move from room to room
—a visitor, a stranger, a friend
imagine myself carrying daffodils

imagine myself bearing good news
imagine myself bringing life
to all that seemed doomed
I am walking at the bottom of the sea
My heart swims above me
like a face I ought to know

That Day at War

I had forgotten
until I wended my way
through the streets
in this northern Iraqi city
how as an adolescent
in Bracebridge
we tossed whiskey bottles
stuffed with lit gasoline-soaked rags
at rotted out tree stumps
and ran like hell
and buried our heads
in the snowbanks
feeling a deafening shudder
in the cold earth
We played soldiers
from the Second World War
borrowed jammed German Lugers
defunct bolt action rifles
and stick grenades
—souvenirs from
other boys' fathers
who came home from the war
We crawled through
the wet underbrush
creeping up on
imaginary enemy lines
and once set fire
to a hermit's shack
in the woods along

the river behind
my father's factory
until one winter
we outgrew such games
took up snooker
at the pool hall
spent days
in the smoke-filled confines
below Main Street
and forgot war and terror
Now I walk this market street
in Northern Iraq, listen
to a man telling me how
his best friend's son
was left bloodied
and dead
on the doorstep
of his house
to make a statement
to register fear
to tell the world
And I wondered about
the poor man whose
house we burned
in the dead of
winter, what kind
of statement that was
what kind of war

RONNIE R. BROWN

Born in Brockton, Massachusetts, Ronnie R. Brown moved as a young woman to Montreal and then Ottawa. *States of Matter* (Black Moss, 2005) won the Acorn-Plantos People's Poetry Award, for which *Night Echoes* (2006), her fifth collection, was also short-listed. This "micro-fictional narrative" is from her forthcoming collection *Rocking on the Edge*.

Heat Exhaustion

I

When they bring her the news
she tries to be sad
just as she did
those times she'd lose a baby—
blood snaking down her legs
cramps coming way too soon. But
all she feels is relief.

An accident
they say. Don't worry, she and the kids
will do okay, there's compensation,
insurance, benefits. Death
benefits. Yes, everything
will be alright.

Alright! She's heard that before.
Seven babies in twelve years, not counting
those that didn't take. Oh,
she'd loved him once, his hands hot on her
body, his breath burning
in her ear, begging, Please, oh please.
Say yes, and I promise
everything will be alright.

So she let his hands
spread their warmth, part
her thighs, change her life. Her father
crying as he walked her down the aisle,
her Sunday dress stretched tight. A wife
at seventeen. A mother
three months later. And he,
still saying over and over
that everything was alright.

Except he hated the factory. Once
he'd had plans—trade school, carpentry, now
there was no time. Babies kept coming,
colicky, big. How many times
had she asked permission,
begged to use something. But the priest
only coughed, his silhouette
outlined through the confessional's mesh.
He'd cough, shake his head and launch into
his set speech. Sin, sacrament,
duty ringing in her ears.

II

She told herself he was
a good husband, or at least
tried to be. Worked overtime
when he could. Of course, he drank up
most of the extra with the boys,
while she waited at home. And often
just when she'd quieted the kids down,
closed her own eyes,
he'd come home, the smell of beer
outpacing him up the stairs. She'd lie
still, try not to hear the bathroom sounds—
grunts, belches, farts, the gush of piss slowing
to a trickle, clothes
dropping to the tiled floor.

She'd pretend to be asleep,
but still he'd climb onto her.
No kisses, not a gentle touch
just up with her nightie
and poke, poke, poke.

The first time
she'd said no, sobbed
till he pushed away. They'd fought
that whole night. Next day
he'd called in sick—a day's pay gone,
and him asleep, while, eyes red,
mind numb, she'd had to get up,
care for the kids.

After that, she just took it.
Body stiff, unmoving,
she'd hold her breath,
count in her head—
one-two-three...until
it was done.

But, even so, she had loved him
once, was, after all,
still his wife. And every now and then
he'd treat her right—touch her,
kiss her, and the heat
would rise, well up
from some hidden place. Then,
for a while, she'd be young again, safe,
warm in his arms, almost forgetting, till
a toddler would shriek, a baby wail.

III

Except the warmth came less
and less. Even when he'd really try,
exhaustion blanketed her nights,
extinguished sparks before
they had the chance to flame.
Now when other factory wives
come around bringing baked goods,
hand-me-downs, sympathy,
she sees the same exhaustion burning
in their faces, knows
she's better off. And
when one or the other asks
if she misses (voice softening
so the children won't hear) the warmth
of a man in her bed,
she cannot answer, will not explain,
simply shakes her head and whispers,
"It's fine like this, really, it's
alright, everything
is quite all right."

ALICE MAJOR

Alice Major has published nine collections of poetry and served as the first Poet Laureate for the City of Edmonton (2005-07). Past president of the League of Canadian Poets, she won both the Pat Lowther Memorial and BPAA "Book of the Year" awards for *The Office Tower Tales* (UAP, 2008). "The Movies" is reprinted by permission of the author from *Memory's Daughter* (UAP, 2010).

The Movies

Persistence of vision

Action sliced so thin it freezes
into a single frame, a picture
in a Zoetrope. Revolving drum,
a slit, a source of light
and the stopped motion re-starts.
The eye reassembles tiny increments
into continuous flow.

A parlour curiosity, Victorian novelty,
those flickering dreams. And yet
the turning drum created
a kind of heat. Hold a strip
of newly invented celluloid nearby
and it bursts into light
around the world, horses dash
across screens as wide as walls.
The feverish crank of cameras,
reels flying through the projector's
thin, bright 'now'. Cowboys,
Cupid's bows and swashbucklers
are animated, twenty-eight frames
per second, the heated friction
of narrative, its persistent visions.

Oh, Rose Marie, I love you

She loved the love stories.
The talkies then so new, younger
than her own young life,
sound printed as a barred scrim
beside the sprocket holes
along a strip of images,
meshing cleverly with movement
as Nelson Eddy belted out the long, strong notes
of *Rose Marie* like a conveyor belt.
Sound drenching landscape
as if it were quite reasonable to fill
Canadian forests with a full-blown orchestra.

Her birthday treat—taken to the pictures
in the afternoon. Rialto Cinema
on College Street, the new film
Maytime. Her grandfather paid down
sixpences for tickets
and they entered the flicker of story
half-way through. Jeannette MacDonald
as the ball's belle, Nelson Eddy waltzing her
around spring-time's ribboned pole.
May enchanted.

They watched until the end, and then
until the point where they came in.
That's it, May, said her granddad.
We've seen it all. But she pleaded
to see that scene again, and then another
until her patient grandfather
got cross and said, *I'm going now.*
You'd better come along.
But she sat there alone
in the palace of repeatable dreams.
Watched to the end
then round again.

For once, the princess had refused
to leave at midnight.
She waltzed home at last, in thrall
to her Presbyterian stepmother's scolds.
But did not care. Her feet were on petals.
She had been to the ball.

Maytime

We bring back *Maytime*, my mother and I,
iridescent
on a DVD's whirling circle.
In the present,
the past lifts from its static, stuttered pattern
of pits in plastic,
the way time's phase transition melts the solid,
inelastic,
into flow with the ruby laser-tip of 'now'.

We watch, content,
the end. The old lady slipping into sleep below
the tanglement
of blossom-laden branches. The young lover's ghost
bending down,
reaching out transparent hands to her.
Music blown
around them like returning swallows—*Sweetheart,
sweetheart, sweetheart,
will you love me always?* And her young self rises
to step apart
from that old, discarded body. She takes his hand,
unhesitating
ghost. A different phase transition—the solid
sublimating
straight to air, something that inhabits neither
solid nor stream,
but time itself—its pattern of pits and lands.

We turn the machine
off. The notes and images have re-condensed
on the silver skin
of the DVD, like a film of quick mercury
coating glass.
I click the disk safely inside the hard fact
of its cover, pass
it to my mother. She takes it, tucks it
in, at random
on the rack below my father's picture.

His sad phantom
still walks a dementia ward nearby,
the lost glow
of shared lives fading from his pitted mind.

Still, we know
that we can watch this tale at least, whenever
we want its hands
held out to us, its springs, its silvered pasts,
its happy ends,

its promised ghosts.

COLIN MORTON

Colin Morton's recent books include *Dance, Misery*; *The Cabbage of Paradise*; *The Merzbook and other poems*; *The Local Cluster*; and *The Hundred Cuts: Sitting Bull and the Major*. He has also published a novel and co-produced the animated sound-poetry film *Primiti Too Taa*. (www3.sympatico.ca/cmorton)

Invitation au voyage

And the lady returned to her husband's chamber
saying *We're not safe here.*

He only wanted me and now he knows
he can't have me let's take French leave.

That's how the old stories begin—in mid-
thread, with a teaser of intrigue. Later

the sword will split the stone, we'll dispose
of the Puce Knight, the whole dramatis personae

—directly or by indirection, that's what we're about
to find out—but hang on, soyons calme.

Let the gaze linger awhile longer
on the figure of the Lady, silvery

in the moonlight flushed with indignation.
The end will be bloody and soon enough.

Why rush to judgment day?
All but one knight will fail, we know from the start

and only in dreams do you wander for a year and
a day and return to the home you left.

The Progressive *Interview*
(Harold Pinter, March 2001)

I don't know. How the hell
can I say what changed my life?
Perhaps all I can tell you is that
at the age of thirteen I fell madly in love
with a girl who lived on my street.
It wasn't her fault, but
I became very unhappy. I mean,
we had a certain kind of relationship,
very young. But I think
the fact she was inevitably going to go on to others
and wasn't going to be mine forever...
I was writing a lot of poetry to do with precisely that.

My father was a tailor, you know.
He used to get up very early to go to work.
One morning he came down and found me
sitting at the kitchen table, writing,
I think I was almost in tears. And he said,
"What are you doing?" quite gruff.
And I said, "I don't know, Dad,
I don't know what I'm doing."

He took what I was writing and looked at it.
Then he gave it back to me
and just patted me on the head and went to work.
He never referred to it again.
He didn't say, "Oh, put that rubbish away,"
or anything like that. He just knew
I was going through the anguish of love.
And I always loved him for that.

Dear Jeremiah

And what if it's true
        your sister did worse?

Most anyone caught in the act
        confesses. But you?

You may have forgotten, child
        but I knew you when you could do no wrong.

So tell me you'll come visit Sunday
        and I'll barbecue a roast.

Even if the flood maroons me here
        I'll leave the light on over the door.

Memento

Themistocles, offered the gift of memory, wished instead for forget-fulness, a gift Funes the Memorious might have cherished too. Funes, as his friend Borges wrote, remembered each detail of every moment of his life, so that he could not understand why a dog standing should be called by the same name as the same dog sitting, much less why two different creatures should both be called dog. In the end, Borges concluded, his inability to forget differences left Funes unable to reason, unable to think.

To help unravel his mystery, the amnesiac Guy Pierce in *Memento* resorted to tattooing key memories into his skin. But the one thing he'd have bargained anything to forget—that memory never ceased tormenting him.

Women forget the pain of childbirth, I am told. If not, we might not be here to wonder about these things, not so many of us anyway. But what if all pain were so readily forgotten? You wouldn't think to take your hand out of the fire, or to dress warmly in winter.

Let forgetfulness be selective then: excise only the tumours of shame that cling to healthy memories—untake-backable things done or said when, as we say, *I wasn't myself*—that may be the one memory some-one has of us.

Whose version is correct, then? Isn't my self my own, to remember or forget? Coming to terms with yourself (I read when first calling myself a writer) means not only facing the mistakes you made but accepting their role in making you who you have become.

> The grave forgets:
> don't go there
> just to think of me.

BETSY STRUTHERS

Betsy Struthers has published nine poetry books and three mysteries. *Still* won the 2004 Pat Lowther Memorial Award for the best book of poetry by a Canadian woman. A former president of the League of Canadian Poets, she lives in Peterborough, Ontario, and works as an editor of academic texts.

Heaven of Touch

"We have / lived so long in the heaven of touch."
—Mary Oliver

Take off your shoes, your woolly
socks. It is time to walk bare foot.

> Ice armadas sail the lake, and
> all the migratory ducks,
> buffleheads, mergansers,
> in twos and fours cruise
> back and forth across the bay.

> All day as we clean the cottage
> sweep out dead flies, air
> pillows and mattresses,
> the phoebe sings his heart out
> from the top of the split maple,
> two notes, her name, accent
> on the first syllable yearning.

> What winter has struck down:
> the white pine on the island toppled
> after 50 years.

Take off your shoes. Let naked feet
caress stubble grass, downy moss,
slick granite. Sun low
over the bare hills, sky cerulean.

> Tip the little urn.
> When she was happy, her tail
> wagged her whole body: here
> by the gatepost, on the hill

69

where the feral lilies grow,
on the rocks along the shore.

Gust of cold air swirls the ashes,
eddies. Take a deep breath.
Call her home for the last time.
Sad, sad. That catches in the throat.

●

My mother
falling.

First when she saw
my brother come to meet us
after three days of vigil.
My sisters and I
could barely hold her up.

And when we closed
Dad's coffin, wait, wait, she
cried out, his heart is still
beating. We led her away,
her knees buckling.

Ten years and she keeps
tripping. A walker
makes no difference, nor
the carpeted hallways
of her new home, its
tidy single room.
All she wants comes to her
in dreams. This is why
she sleeps all day. Why
her eyes close when
she hugs us. When we
turn our cheeks
to her parched lips.

We are obliged by all
that is good in us to give
the beloved pet release. She
is too weak to lift her head
as the pink narcotic
drips into her vein.
I hold her to the end,
which is not bitter.

All I can do
for my mother
is listen, is hug

though I have to
turn my back
when she kneels
at his grave

the stone solid, unmoving,
his name carved
by her raw fingers.

We are a family trained
not to give in to tears.
To shake hands and
buck up. We have no
template for this: the
yearning to be touched.

In the conservatory, she
pushes her walker
past photographers
and strollers. The incense
of hyacinth, narcissus
wash over her, she
does not stop. She is a bear

in her mink coat, wakened
too soon from hibernation,
the dream that he is calling
for her, that he waits
on the other side of the
hothouse door. Perhaps
in the cactus room,
the crown of thorns.

*

Easy for me, you can say it,
to get another dog, they're going begging
in kennels and pounds.

    Pick up the puppy, handful
    of need. So hard to put her down.
    Soon I will bring this puppy home,
    my lapdog, little muse.

And easy for me, she can say it,
to come home to you, beside me
all the sleepless nights

    when worries chase their tails.
    I want to shake her eyes open: look,
    here is the world and it is ours
    for such a little while.

In the manicured garden, the plum tree
is in blossom. Sit. Sit facing
the spring sun's benediction.

    My turn will come. Palms
    held open, a cup to catch
    white petals falling.

RACHAEL SIMPSON

Rachael Simpson won the 2009 Lilian I. Found poetry prize from Carleton University for "Heirlooms," which was then published in *In/Words* Magazine. She lives in Kingston, Ontario.

Heirlooms

I

A garden does not grow blue china
chicken bones or brass keys
but all of these
found when the soil turns over,
times when the hoe can't go
any farther.

Mother pulled a teaspoon
out of the ground.
Told me to wash it
for supper.

II

A clearing does not begin a garden
just as a house does not begin a home.
It must be lived in,
plotted
sown.

My mother's garden
was first a hole
dug for the outhouse,
a place to throw
the kitchen scraps.

I often think of this
when squatting in the dirt,
dusting the heirloom tomatoes.

JOHN B. LEE

John B. Lee lives in Port Dover. He has published 50 books and received 60 awards, including the Acorn-Plantos People's Poetry Award (three times), the CBC Literary Award, and the Eric Hill Award. In 2005 Lee was inducted as Poet Laureate of Brantford in perpetuity.

The Summer My Son Painted the House

The summer
I insisted that my unemployed son
paint the house
he rattled up the ladder
arriving at all the windows at once
his swung pail clangouring
like anger in an orchard
and all that white paint tainted the panes
splashed the sill and
dashed at the brick
as he came swathing toward the sashes
like ledge pigeons
like rock gulls, like guano
at the cenotaph
like bird lime
on the hero's stony forehead in the park
oh, he was dutiful enough
to do it
but his disgruntlement at being forced
wept from his every pore like milk
and he was furious
his bristled arms whisked like dog wag, like sea splash
and when he came to me
wanting recompense
his white hands still wet
his body half-bleached
as if he were slowly but surely
becoming Master Blank
or as if he were an old soul becoming 'the boy'
face first...

and looking much like
the son in the photograph album
the son on my desk dipped to the chin
in lilies
the one I loved
who isn't so angry
who when I sell this house some day
as one might sell
the brick of swans
the glaze of some fog-drowsy
window cleaner
smearing the glass with soap
in gone-dry splotches
that suffer the yard to blur
I also sell off little
tints of wrath—oh buyer
think of yourself as
Vincent's brother Theo
this mason's canvas as a living record
these windows
descended from angels
whose shoulders rubbed off a chalky beatitude
flying in, flying out
and my son was simply
tracing their journey
their sojourn lingering in frost

Why Are Manholes Round

I play shinny
with the oldest man on ice
a shaky skater
an octogenarian wobbler
barely erect on shivery blades
he stands alone
frozen in place
like a thin-ice pylon

his stick like a bent cane
tapping a wooden code
avoid avoid avoid
and someone says
"draw a circle round him
see if he moves…"

he's what you might call
without intent of flattery
"a stay at home defenseman"
for some say "he should stay at home"
but there he is always
tracing the varicose blue of the paint below ice
to the left-most half of himself
as if he were salting the line
to be sure of it there

and when others sweep past
saying "skate like the wind, not skate like you're winded"
down comes his shaft in their wake
with a chop to the ribs or the arms or the shins
down like a hospital parking-lot gate
on the trunk
or the hood
a move he denies
though it's feckless of hurt
as a blow from the willowy dead

once he was caught on film
tripping a fellow
with steel in both wrists
so his victim fell with a clank
and was slow to get up
as iron too heavy to lift from the pig
with both his brave knees
gone awonk

and still, dear Davey denied
though he'd been seen on the ice
and caught by the camera
and watched and confirmed by the room
sweeping both feet following through
still he said, "that wasn't me!"
and, "I did not!"
like a felon red-handed in court.

I remember the night
he'd spent
all day sledging a floor
so it cracked
into wedges of broken concrete
like a river's first thaw
which he lifted and wheeled
by himself in the ache of the hours
and still he came out to play
though his arms were dead as wet gravel
and his legs
were as weak as fat sand
yet he laced up his ankles
and walked like a three-legged chair

I suppose he might pass
through the thinnest of glaze
one night he'll capsize
the ink of his blades
carving through
as a child on a pond
in the give of first cold
to go down
where the water won't freeze
and he'll skate like a fish
with his fins to the sky   under ice

Erín Moure

Erín Moure is a Montreal poet and translator who writes mainly in English, albeit multilingually. Her most recent books are *O Resplandor* (Anansi, 2010) and—in collaboration with Oana Avasilichioaei—*Expeditions of a Chimœra* (Book Thug, 2009). "Executive Suite" is from *Sheepish Beauty: Civilian Love* (Véhicule, 1992), and is reprinted with permission of the author. See Notes, p. 153.

Executive Suite

1) Apperception

Sometimes having no sense of what is terrible,
we are blinded by this, the immediate apperception of the site
as (im)mediate surface, the ripples off the side of Place Ville Marie
City of Mary
Place or site of Mary, the city, ripples off the side of the cruciform tower &
smaller towers coincident upon it,
the offices of Air Canada & Quebec Tourism, the open plaza with its
concrete
structures, the im(moderate) resistance of the earth to structure,
underneath ther is probably

forested memory patterns in the soil, we exist
on top of this, having no sense of what is terrible
in our own lives

the woman in the blue skirted suit & white luminescent blouse,
patterned
with flowers, who exists within the paradigm only as solidified
blue suit & white luminescent blouse patterned with flowers,
a bit of the air solidified into image of
blue suit & white luminescent blouse patterned with flowers

the other woman, who doesn't care to be represented is represented
as black space, which will get her nowhere, they
(speech-chutterers, speaking,
the always-speaking, the freedome of this,
free speech, in these plazas

2) Co-incident

The light co-incident upon the concrete sheen of the towers, the high
windows
& internal ventilation, bringing upward into the executive floors
diesel smoke of the train station
It is the underground city
It is the blue blouse & white luminescence of the woman
"in transition"
thinking the obedient shelf-life of hunters, thinking
the blue jeep & co-incident reflection of male example,
which is here in the executive site
the referent to which all signals are matched for thoroughness
of structure

To work here is a thin breeze chilling the chest
To work here is a thin strand of mucous pulled out of the veins
To work here is a sore neck & brilliant tensity
Carrying the paper from desk to file,
holding it upward,
the other woman not luminescent
but wearing black, burning the page, incorporate
Her cruciform body an operative extension of certain screens,
word-processing

To tell you the truth, it stinks.
It exactly stinks.
The luminescent as a way of speaking. Not a stutter.
The active dress.

3) *Paradigm*

Because it is an old movie, the other woman says,
I wear the colour of smoke or warehouses or
black holes into which all matter is sucked &
becomes its negative
Where does the surface go when we are speaking, the anti-
surface, the "below"
I have to watch her when I use words, her boss chuckles,
she stands holding the page, ready to burn it
literally because it will not light
By ignoring it
By showing it has no content
By deconstruction which certain poets claim has no use in reality
The real world
This is it, Bronwen
The page is on fire, now

The sky's light off the cruciform tower, the shields of roof reconstructed
in the city's plaza, the famous light place in the centre of a city, from
which the mountain is visible, it is modernism in the *pays* of bent stairs,
its concrete similarity to parks, to *park-like*, our forested subcutaneous
layers shining dull into our partisan eyes, us from *station McGill* into the
wide street sainted alley, the way into the Place Ville Marie, city of Mary,
apperceptive surface in our own lives

This is it, the other woman says
her black coat turning
the page gone

4) Analog*

Already a lifetime use of the word "small" has worn me out of
description.
Like this, she said, like this.
Feeling the calcified deposits forming around the heart, she
stood up & shuffled, restless with coffee.
Oh, murder, that curse.
The small cup, the small towel, the small slice of tomato.

As if the words in any kitchen. Place
two eggs on the plate, & arrange the potatoes before service.
Collateral for a small
heart is a small job following instructions.

"The heart tick of the alarm" is a quote from, from, from.
She gets up to the micro noise, & the ventilation. The
roof of a famous building in Montreal.
Three pages this Wednesday.
Train them how to speak of the "club meal," the man said.
Oh murder, that curse. She gets up, restless,
the bone worn in her hands from touching, the computer.
She remembers the dial telephone.
She remembers the steam gauge, registering on a good day, 160 pounds.
She remembers placing the eggs on the plate, in the metal kitchen, the three
slices of bacon, garnished with
tomato one year, orange the next, now
they speak of melon, & she dreams of

celery. Not on the plates, but
in the field behind the woman's house, plowed up, the sun just up over
the lake, late summer & the first cold, her black clothes beside the bed, shorn,
& in that field, so many stalks of celery.

---

* To proceed by inference from the known to the unknown. Just as in a watch, the
hands refer to, but are not, the passage of time. If we refer to the unknown, are we not
placing it already into a representational framework that perhaps fails to represent
it? It is said in answer that the poem must remain "full of holes." As if the leaks, that
absorb matter, are the places where the real poem is. We create the respresentation in
language not to mirror reality but as a physical relation by which the leaks are visible.

5) *Cruciform*

The poem ends with a traditional plea to Mont Royal

Oh mountain with yr turd & horse clop, smell of maple
Oh mountain with yr Torah paths & condom papers
yr rock & soil, yr sexual secretions
From yr concrete lookout, eye to generations, snow-blown, visible
structures of downtown, Place Ville Marie or l'Édifice Radio Canada,
the woman in blue luminescent shoulders, speaking the voice of hunters
& illimited shelf life, speaking the incorporate behind those windows,
luminescent sheen stepping upward, concrete torpor where the wind is
twisted, (im)moderate surface, represented as cruciform tower, city of
Mary, a surface we speak

to be comprehens(ible), to smile & kiss each other,
the towers perceptible in our body's surfaces,

the women in blue suit & white blouse patterned flowers

the women in blue clothes incorporate speaking

our faces, shorn

CORRECTIONS: "Executive Suite"

The poem lacks simple narration. Simple narration is absent and it doesn't work to make a mystical image out of celery, even as a joke. Jokes are improper in poems, even if people know they are jokes, and why should this be a joke. Not to mention contesting your friends. The reference to Bronwen seems to be a personal, private reference to a conversation that did not include the reader. The poem is not the place for E-Mail. The forested memory patterns appear and vanish forever. The spelling of the word "ther" is deliberate and will be questioned in Toronto. The mountain appears in an idiotic parody of A. M. Klein that is deadly serious and not parody at all. It is modern honouring of one's forebears. He lived in a house something like this one and, after several years, ceased going to his law office at all. Or when he did, he would look down on rue Ste. Catherine at the people passing and not touch a word of law. All this is imagination, I renounce it publicly to avoid lawsuits from his estate. One of his sons is a lawyer whose office is in Place Ville Marie. In the spring the leaves take a long time to come out on the mountain, the maple. I dream instead those western aspens whispering and their bright smell. We both have lived near the Mont Royal. In the spring the leaves take a long time, and we ache and ache until it happens. He died of a heart attack in his sleep in 1972. The corrections rely too much on the body of the poem. It is not a correction. Before the Catholic writer can give homage to the Jew she must come to terms with Pope Pius signing the Concordat with Hitler. What good are corrections in this case. There are some things uncorrectable, except with the mouth. We are going deep into the Metro, bearing the leaves we dream of, this spring.

1985

Appetite

MONTY REID

Ottawa poet Monty Reid has published 13 collections of poetry. Honours include three nominations for Governor-General's Awards, Alberta's Stephansson Award for Poetry (three times), and the Lampman-Scott Award. Until recently, he was Director of Exhibitions at the Canadian Museum of Nature. He plays guitar and mandolin in the group Call Me Katie.

Patois

1. Incompatible

inevitable
        as taxes

you are held
        in the jargon
                we project and overrun

unaccountable
        the expense nobody could predict.

once I thought it could be written
        off
                that you could enter love
                across from income
        and everything would balance
                        out

that the books could be explained.

        it almost broke us.
now I hunt through your body
        for deductions
                invest in forgotten islands

        claim the heart

        and keep my receipts
           for years.

2. *Spatial Form*

breath

        breaks you

                apart

       as a lovers

         quarrel, domestic

            spat

                in which you need

                    the last word

how you get up and leave the room

      and the air collapses

          in the space of

             your disappearance

and how return trembling

      to each other

         to our impractical selves

            and know this form

              is a body

       and I am breathing

        heavy.

3. *Patience Plant*

because the globes of nectar

        hung sweetly on its blossoms

the kids loved this plant

        they touched the petals and said

it grew sugar and I told them don't

     touch, it kills

the flowers, but you said plants

      like it, sing

to them

and when later I thought it got
its name for its own slow
    growth you said no

everything else waits for it, look
    how the kids have grown up attending
it, how it has grown evenly and

    a sweetness still hangs in
its blossoms, look how the light waits
    constantly at the window

        you said
            turning the pot around.

4. Appattite

names have to do with hunger and
hunger is a misspelt word

names misunderstand the stomach
but that's natural. raw

oysters. the hand tightening
upon air when you try to pet the cat

and the cat vanishes.
after we went out for dinner

at a Spanish restaurant and came
home and made love on Dombsky's

narrow bed. that was the night
I cut my foot on the mirror tile.

hunger is the way your body
closes upon mine and there is no

vanishing. how Dombsky hoped we were
still close because we would be in that

bed. how I bled all over the glass
in my sleep. the morning

holds so tightly. it smells of oysters and
garlic butter and has a sore foot

and we have never been so loosened
into the ordinary world as in the

body's spell. this present magic
makes the apparition real.

and I am cut by a surface that in
theory should be perfectly flat.

5. *Spatula*

the omelette of dreams
folds in on
itself

　　　ah, French cuisine

the genuine
article
there at the end
of the handle you proffer

what is given is the real
thing

and you scoop up the whip
of egg, pepper, tomato, onion
set it on the plate

　　　and on the table

　　　　　precise

　　　flowers
　　　in a jar

MARY DALTON

Mary Dalton is the author of four volumes of poetry, recently *Merrybegot* and *Red Ledger*. A letterpress chapbook, *Between You and the Weather*, was released by Running the Goat Books in 2008. Dalton lives in St. John's, and teaches at the Memorial University of Newfoundland. See Credits, p. 153, for sources of "The Swallowing" and "Vertical Panel."

After Basho

Even in Gallows Cove,
hearing the snipe winnowing,
I'm longing for Gallows Cove.

The Swallowing

Rumour is,
that one in the corner,
she's up from Georgia for the summer.
Hot, Georgia, and steamy.

Rumour is,
he was ossified;
he staggered out of the tavern and fell in a river.

Rumour is,
she laughed as they squared off, she the
proud prize for the victor, the buyer of beer.

Rumour is,
he lurched out of the beer parlour, toppled over the wharf—
the tide gave him back later.

Rumour is,
under the red-hot lights of the dance floor
she clasped him close to her; that night
they each found a way out of the muttering dark.

Rumour is,
lots of jobs down north,
big money down north. Or
big jobs down south, lots of
money down south.

Rumour is,
he climbed up into the antlered light fixture;
when the cops came, he roared down, in his falsetto,
Watch out now—I'll gut the place!

Rumour is,
before the crash
the police held him up twice that night,
didn't take his keys. He'd passed the breathalyzer,
walked a straight line.

Rumour is,
she was knocking them back, her sons stuck in the car;
the ten-year-old, in the rear, deep in comics,
wriggled into the front, saved them the both of them:
jammed on the brake after the three-year-old
fiddled with the gearshift, headed them out towards the water.

Rumour is,
buddy took off for the mainland;
now she's anyone's for the price of a vodka.

Rumour is,
the cocaine is crack, the poker game's fixed,
the dealer's a narc, the jukebox is broken.

Rumour is,
that one's drowning a sorrow,
that one's fleeing a demon. Here
the shadows are warming; here
there's always a story to accompany
the swallowing.

Vertical Panel
(Cento, line 2)

She'd been identifying patterns:
first one doesn't come back, and then another and another,
so it is natural that they should drown,
the large expected gods.

The little potter's sponge called an "elephant ear,"
it had no trouble accepting its limits,
given the night
in the indiscriminate green.

A puppy laps the water from a can,
bites its own tail: a New Year starts to choke.
Moon-fingers lay down their same routine:
goosedown like thrown boas of a chorus line.

The language of trees. That's done indoors—
the wild caprices and bouts of pulse
weave and dive like Stukas on their prey,
the darting thing in the pile of rocks.

Say your life broke down. The last good kiss
which takes place in a room
where the legs intertwine to keep the body warm—
exhibits for the Museum of Humanity.

Later, a delayed moon. And a violent moon
stands every fibril of the mind on end;
hangs there helplessly, but doesn't drop
except where one black-haired tree slips.

Who says? A nameless stranger,
American or Canadian.
A vertical panel with him in it—
and the polar bear, is he here too?

What Came

Awkward Alba, hunched over
an old orange-crate desk. Rain
riffed easy along the roof;
then a lunatic moon shed its grief
through the window. She
was, it might be, setting out
in a poem words that would net
a glimpse, or faint spoor,
of the shy beast named Love.

She was expecting Cupid to drop in,
that petulant boy, so careless
with toys. Or Aengus,
dreamy-eyed after travels. Or
Heathcliff, or Dracula, their capes flung back
to reveal the red lining
as thunder roared, bolts carved up the sky.

What came, though, was quieter:
the arc of a hand as it pulled
thread through a needle, drew
a paintbrush across pitted walls;
a shoulder taut in the hoisting
a bed-frame, wrought-iron, up stairs.

BLAINE MARCHAND

Ottawa writer Blaine Marchand has published a young-adult novel and six poetry books; honours include the Lampman-Scott award. A former President of the League of Canadian Poets, he co-founded Ottawa Independent Writers, the Ottawa Valley Book Festival, and *Sparks* magazine. These poems are from *The Craving of Knives* (Buschek, 2009).

The Pale Object of Desire

Sleep weights the body,
like the Rift Valley wall,
between sheets and cover.
At the deepest point,
the moon floats above the rim.
Sometimes ridged fingers
of an inclined hand.
Sometimes the pale plain
between a rise of hip bones.
Sometimes hair drifting
across a face.

Deep within the body,
desire is an ancient land
nomads wander through
and never possess;
is a water catchment
drawn to the surface
of the parched savannah.

The tropic sun
slides under the eyelids,
dissolves.
But traces remain,
stippled with moisture.
Morning light whets ·
the canopies of acacia,
douses the leafless baobabs
like hairs on the folds
of far-off hills,
like down matted
at the torso's divide.

night's blind

you are not here, and even
when you are, you are distant,
your body withheld

withholding, stifling
small cries, refusing
the pleasure points

of my fingers. the dark
thread, night's blind
behind which you watch

my voice wants
to fly up and scatter
in a smattering of words

like birds tearing themselves
from the skin of ice
but fear follows, fells me

fear of deficiency, of speech
or having spoken, the shunning silence,
the body after its last breath

the body once held and taken
into the mouth, now just skin
cold and unyielding

concealed
loss of faith, faithfulness,
abundance abandoned

lashed by winter winds
white squall, the flurry
wings pummeling, flight

where, where are you?
and why
these shards, disguised images—

a footprint rutted on a shoreline,
an unmarked grave,
a bird cleaved of its tongue?

Void

All night long, drifting
in and out of sleep. The fan
a hand trying to lift my skin.

Earlier, in a crypt
the ancient tour guide bent down,
with thumb and forefinger
raised a leathery flap
of stomach, the remains
of an old Coptic nun at peace
for 500 years. Inside,
her kidneys, liver, spleen brown
as stones that the ocean deposits
in a hidden bay.

All night long,
vendors swarm in market streets
tug at my shoulders, arms, wrists,
all night,
a young black girl, the empty basket
of her eyes crusted with rheum,
fingers exploring
her cavity of mouth,
nearby, a Tureg man in a jade turban,
flicking up the lid
of a camel-hide coffer,
inside, boxes dyed
maroon, emerald, ebony,
hollow
spaces in a sunken chest
I can't breathe

drift in and out
unsettled,
searching for
somewhere inside,
a void
where I can be
mortared, brick by brick.

MARILYN GEAR PILLING

Hamilton writer Marilyn Gear Pilling is the author of two collections of short fiction and four books of poetry, and her writing has won and been shortlisted for many national awards, recently including *Arc*'s Poem of the Year (Editor's Choice) and *Descant*'s Winston Collin's Best Canadian Poem award (first place).

Four Days before Christmas

Dusk rises from the ground outside my window,
O Magnum Mysterium rises
from the speakers on the high-shelved
books of this room and the snow
keeps coming, big buffeting gusts this afternoon,
now the flakes falling
vertical as a beanpole in a folk tale,
hundreds of feathery snow poles stretching
from heaven to earth, and as dusk thickens
into dark, I can just make out
the dead, sliding down, sliding down, one after another.

The dead I say. My dead I mean. Every year
at this time, more of them.
My parents and their kin,
the country folk of East Wawanosh,
all that generation,
their hands ingrained with toil,
bodies ruled by the quickening green spears
of transformation in spring,
the dwindling every fall.
Colleagues whose half-lived lives
dangle behind like the severed tail of a kite, its body
lost in high blue. And last,
after a long pause, and still in the coal-dark
hoodie she wore to the train tracks,
Stéphanie.

        My dead. Invisible in the falling
snow. I can feel them out there; I know
what they want. They want
the rich dark sauce of Christmas
on their tongues, they want to tell me

what they've learned in their
discarnate lives, they want in and I want
them in, want to tell them how they go on
changing, even in death.
           Longing arrows
        from them to me and back again, almost
cracks the cold pane.

Tune

Here, the night chitters softly along the dark lagoon.
  In the distance, a woman's voice cries an old

song, her Spanish frays into the ocean's uneasy
    coming and going. Under my breastbone a wistful

tune breaks over and over.

Two thousand miles north, you sit at your window.
  Little coils of snow come and go

on the bare road. You write that the tree you
    described last week as wearing

a golden dress late-lit down her side
    is memory now.

Here, the lagoon. Its mystery, its deep. Silent shape
  of a waiting catamaran

on its dark body. The lagoon, its quiet breathing,
the streak on its surface where the

moon breaks over and over.

CAROLYN SMART

Carolyn Smart's fifth collection of poems, *Hooked—Seven Poems*, was published in 2009 by Brick Books. An excerpt from her memoir *At the End of the Day* won first prize in the 1993 CBC Literary Awards. She founded the RBC Bronwen Wallace Award for Emerging Writers, and teaches Creative Writing at Queen's University, Kingston.

the trials of Cumie Barrow

born in Nacogdoches, small girl of the hardshell kind
I was tough, raised right by the cane &
did not paint my face

I joined right up with Henry & his dream to own a farm,
the right & Christian way to live

we worked in bone-dry fields that gave us back so little
but knew we would endure

I birthed seven children one by one &
each survived the plagues of youth & fortune
till the bad days came

it was earnest work at first,
planting on those rented acres
& then it turned plain rough I have to say
hiring out to other farms to eat

worked indoors just as hard
shacks & tents & underneath a wagon
my children by my side

just held my head up straight
& kept my hands in use
I'll be no devil's playground

here's what I'd do each day:
work the fields, mind babies,
fix the dinner, wash the endless filthy clothes,
haul water, nurse the sick
I did what must be done

kept my grim mouth shut
there was no time for dreaming in those days

Henry'd say you make that child mind,
& yes I did: I made them children dance
when rod came out to play

a deep & scrabbling need's what
made me burn from dawn to dusk
so when they sent my boy Buck down
for years
I knew it was not right

hitched up the wagon & picked our way out there
the youngest still so small
she could not pull her weight
three weeks it took us without money

I knew that judge would lean in my direction
my Buck freed before his time
I would have done most anything for him
for all of them, I would not bend

I wrote & begged the judge for Clyde's
swift freedom from the farm
he chopped his toes before he got the word
forever limped & wounded, true mark of the law

I did not care for wayward women
boys with moonshine in their hands
they drew near all my children
& one by one they fell away to sin
I cannot fault their hopes
we were the lowest of the low

nights I'd put my knees down on the hard swept floor
could only pray for some release
exhaustion was our one companion

I could just try to serve them well
to wash their broken bodies
& then lay them in the ground
from dust to dust
you will not see me weep

Pain
(two triolets)

1. Bonnie

burned clear through to bone
she only called out for her mother
did then all it was I could
burned clear through to bone
we cut her from the leaking car
saw the singeing glow of providence
burned clear through to bone
she only called out for her mother

2. Blanche

I wasn't afraid anymore
I saw Buck fall and ran to him
could see inside his brain
I wasn't afraid anymore
the glass tore into both my eyes
there was no sound but gunfire
I wasn't afraid anymore
I saw Buck fall and ran to him

when we drive this way

when we drive this way I like to watch the blur of trees in the dusty
day, the way they turn to blue at a certain hour and I brush my hand
across the cotton skirt to feel the hips rise up against my fingertips,
we drive so long and fast I forget I wear my bones some days

when we stop in the cool of the shade bumping through the low
brush and into a hidden spot Clyde takes out the blanket and spreads
it atop the dry grass, wild carrot lazy in the air on either side and the
sun low romance, makes me pull my hair down smooth across my
cheeks, plump up my beret

he opens the door to me, the brown of his eyes so dark, his small
hand slips behind my back and one beneath my knees so slow the
pain still there and then I'm up and tuck my head below the door
and out into the hot still air hoping for some breeze

we lie upon the blanket, eat the beans and maybe find some little
scraps of meat, share it out with care there is so little now and I know
I am not the pretty thing I used to be, how long will he still love me
when I look like this

he says I am a liar and always sweet but he is that way, only, I do love
him so, when will we die and will it be together right away or will
there be some long slow time of grief, a vast and haunting dream

BRUCE MEYER

Bruce Meyer is author of 30 books of poetry, short fiction, non-fiction and pedagogy, most recently *Dog Days* and *Mesopotamia*. He is professor of English at Georgian College where he teaches for Laurentian University. His broadcasts on literature are the CBC's best-selling spoken word CD series. He lives in Barrie, Ontario.

Gingerbread House

Overhanging the eaves
a white lip of fondant
almost wants to smile

as you press gum drops
around the door to light
a path for travelers.

It's always snowy winter
for houses of gingerbread.
A dusting of icing sugar

over a printless threshold
suggests they sleep inside
or, hard at work baking,

mix lives with stories
that soon are eaten up.
It's a good day to stay in,

to put a roof over dreams,
keep them warm, protect
them from passing storms,

let rise a breath of incense,
as you draw a pan of walls
from the open mouth of love.

Dinner Roll
for Kerry

I love to watch how you
select one from a basket

the way an egg charmer
coddles an Easter surprise.

And as you curl your hand
around its global girth

as if to say the whole world
is there in your warm palm,

I know what it is to love;
to be with you for a meal.

When you broke it open,
I saw how our love tried

to fill the void between
each half, each body now

separate as if miles apart.
I wake in a distant city.

Lights in the window
are unfamiliar. The bed

still holds my body's shape,
a crescent where your teeth

have bitten off the better half.

Bread on Water

It is harder to tell the difference
between my kayak paddle dipping
and my hand trailing in the current
as the afternoon grows timeless...

fingers and waters ringing them
are cool in the tall reflected nimbi
sprouting reeds at ease so gracefully
among red wings on rushed banks.

Slice and flash of sunlit droplets,
the silver paddle song is not a lie,
as momentarily our strokes unison
until you leave me in my time.

Turning far downstream, the dam
mumming the flow, you call to me—
something of my grandmother's lilt
echoes like decades in your girlhood.

I see myself on the Thomas Rennie,
pulsing across Toronto Harbour,
the city shrinking like a cowardly crowd.
My Nana scatters crusts for the ducks.

By the time we reach the still lagoons,
interwoven like fingers in a handclasp
of mirrored willows on Algonquin Island,
she's struck a truce between the season

and time's untenable liquid flow,
calling only to vanish in perfect pitch,
the Irish in her voice fading to silence,
as my kayak edges softly into yours,

and the sky in the Kagawong River
opens to uphold you as if a yellow bird,
the wings of our paddles almost clasped,
as we drift together until I let you go.

BEN LADOUCEUR

Ben Ladouceur lives in Ottawa. His poetry has appeared in the *Claremont Review*, *Bywords Quarterly Journal*, and *Ottawater*, and the chapbooks *Alert* (Angel House) and *The Argossey* (Apt. 9), and has been shortlisted for the John Newlove Poetry Award and George Johnston Poetry Prize (twice).

there were going to be words

i

there were going to be words

since orphaned in the gap

between all of my great lakes and your
isle of man

in the midst of themselves,
defeated

too tiny for funerals

we had to mourn in the crannies
of our lives:

on long car rides
between the meal and its dishes

ii

I wanted for instance to use the word
allele

to describe the things my mother gave me
and my father and then
the things I, lonesome and male, earned

ate the bones, declined
the games of cards

and what are the leftovers
of my little life
what is there to show for it?

iii

there was to be, too, a warning
about the men

who wait outside
me like a house

they ring the doorbell of me
dirty the carpet of me with their muddy feet

their feet
fill me with stink

you can smell them because the molecules
slide into your nostrils and fill niches

I would love to bathe these men
pick their brains

but they won't let me see them in the nude

iv

a memory occurs
with the rudeness of lightning bolts

the nipples that seemed somehow on the brink
of slipping right off

the cinema that was empty but I swear to God
was not, I had company
a dark and sneezy ghost

the food that kept coming

meanwhile,
in the world that is actual

I stand in line for pizza
folk become more blotto and more

somebody threatens to call the cops
but does not

a woman looks like she's going to
vomit but does not

PITH & WRY

MARGARET ATWOOD

Margaret Atwood has written some 40 books of poetry, fiction, and critical essays, and received multiple Canadian and international honours, including the Man Booker, Giller, Dan David, Premio Mondello, and Governor General's awards. She lives in Toronto. These poems first appeared in *Branching Out* (1973, preview issue); see Notes, p. 153.

Chaos poem

i

I return to the house,
the lights are on, you aren't here,

damp towels on the chairs, cat fur
matted in corners, dishes

eaten off, crusted,
books abandoned and bent open;

it looks as though you've just moved out,
but it always looked like that.

ii

Don't worry, I won't cut
anything, I won't leave

sloppy red messages for you
on the bathroom floor.

The fact is I don't like pain,
I don't have that kind of energy,

I'm getting fat,
scenarios wipe me out

in advance and my wrists are lazy.

iii

I lie on the mattress; re-
playing the man trudging
through the snow, hunting

for his enemy / which is the snow
looking for something to shoot
and finding nothing / I rehearse again

the polite and terrible slogans
by which we live (no matter
how courageous failure is failure)

This is not eviction.
I wish you would shut up.

iv

I wash my hair
which gives me the illusion of safety.

You're going and you hate going
as much as you hated staying here.

The rest of my life
is not what you imagine.

I stay awake, listening
to the right half of my skull, spinning
its threads of blood.

I have started
to forget, at night I can hear
death growing in me like a baby with no head.

Life mask

I'm flat on the table, open
side up, they pour white earth
over me, my skin goes under.

Don't move. Breathe slowly. Heavy
and warm, the head is rounded
on both sides now, a melon,

cocoon, I'm plastered up like a hole, a thing
that's been broken. Operation,
repair, my closed mouth
packed in bandages or snow.

O to be frozen. But it
burns, this transformation.
Fold my hands, wait: no angels. Voices
circle me as though I'm not here,

this is it, absence
of love at last, I'm invisible,
I listen to the mourners
depart, shuffling
boots and gloves in the hall.

No such luck. They sit me up, split
my skull in two, I stand

and grope to the sink
to wash death out of my eyes, un-
regenerate, my hollow

face discarded on the chair,
thrown into time like a footprint.

ROGER NASH

Roger Nash is the first Poet Laureate of the City of Greater Sudbury, a past-President of the League of Canadian Poets, and Professor Emeritus in the Philosophy Department of Laurentian University. His seventh poetry collection is *Something Blue and Flying Upwards: New and Selected Poems* (YSP, 2006).

Turning the Tables

Spring

Jellyfish surface
inside the moon's reflection.
Skies can sting to death.

Summer

Bullfrogs puff their cheeks.
Thunder croaks. Lightening flickers
its white tongue at flies.

Fall

On a cloudy night,
potatoes boil in the pan:
full moons for supper.

Winter

Snow falls. By mid-day,
a single snowman has built
dozens of children.

Constants

After a man rose from the dead, toppling
laws of biology, vigorous Crusades
in his name upheld the unchanging laws
of butchery.

After the six million were reduced
to dust, their prayers to particles pilgrimaging
through air and earth, the mass of the planet
remained completely unchanged. Light
still travelled at just the speed of light,
whether puddles it bounced off were water or blood.

After each new generation of mothers
gives birth, in Chicago, Baghdad or Jerusalem,
fresh dreams presenting between their thighs,
and the night-sky glittering with innumerable eels
like the salty stars of an inland sea,
the gravitational pull of the moon and its unceasing
tides remain just the same.
Water still boils at one hundred degrees centigrade,
whether the kettles are blackened and dented, or not.

Whether steam from our kettles keens or sings.

My Father's Laugh

He laughed with a bared hurricane of teeth.
Fallen angels were suddenly covered
with scales, and leaping fish with feathers,
in a world where everything, for the child I was,
now dovetailed, surprisingly but comfortingly,
with everything else—like crabs that overlap in their bucket.
Outside, woodpeckers plucked harps
in the trees, and tar in the street began to smell
of fresh strawberries. Swallows flew
far higher, even, than their disappearing
reflections down the bottom of our well.
Afterwards, with tears in his ankle-deep eyes,
his smile was as happy as wheat-fields.

Amber

A chunk of amber, in the future, will show
what we've preserved, like a fly surprised
in the landslide of its life. Guitars full of explosions,
not honey and song. Roosters that crow
like melted trombones. Church-bells
untolled in fallen steeples, or drowned
in wet sacks of sand. Factories
as inoperable as shoals of fish with cancerous
eyes. Fallen vegetable-carts
in the market, trampled flowers and smiles.
In the chunk of amber, caught forever:
the latest mine disaster, with five
men flattened into one, and buried,
under a comradely group-name, in a single
coffin—that is filled with amber light.

Knitting

On stormy nights, when the power went out,
my grandmother peered for the glasses on top
of her head, to search for the matches held,
in anticipation, in her alert, mole-covered hand.
But she already saw, with perfect vision,
the candle-flame that she wanted to light.
After the tenth grand-child, wish
accomplishes the thought. Needles clicked
to crescendos by themselves while she took a nap.
The day after she died, it seemed they still
hadn't stopped. No endings
are acceptable while there's still wool left.
Her knitting went on uninterrupted, beyond sleep,
beyond power-failures, beyond time ticking in the rusty
clock. Now, when I visit her headstone,
words blurred by the rain and the moss,
I read, as much with wish as with sight,
the fitting tribute: "In knitting we trust."

Sister Amabilis

"When I get tired of praying,
I can always look at the sea."

In the retirement home for nuns, she's still
given to prayer; was given as a young
girl. But its offices, now, are preparatory
to the final office of each day:
what the sea says ceaselessly, ceaselessly.

In this small room, time has been successfully
eroded. The incoming tide, today,
is like the incoming tide yesterday, not late
or soon, or significantly Wednesday, not Tuesday.
It's here to accompany what's unalterable in her smile.

The seven old dunes on the shore,
their marram grass too, are smoothed and ousted.
A maid brings in the afternoon tea.
Steam puffs from the tea-pot's kneeling
spout, neither delayed nor early.

Waves tell the bottle-green beads
of her rosary. There's no particular day
she could die, no more Thursday than Friday.
Lines of foam in the bay will write
her obituary as, simultaneously, the notice of her birth.

Both, like the tides, become indistinguishable, unfailing.

JEANETTE LYNES

Jeanette Lynes' fifth poetry collection is *The New Blue Distance*. Her first novel, *The Factory Voice*, was long-listed for the Scotiabank Giller Prize, and was a *Globe and Mail* Book of the Year. She co-edits *The Antigonish Review* and teaches at St. Francis Xavier University in Antigonish, Nova Scotia.

Thinking of you during security screening at Calgary Airport

My bra sets off the alarm—
O shocking bosom!
Love, you'd laugh at the serious
Official wanding my chest,
you know, my criminal holder,
limp and harmless
as an old basset hound,
a sports bra, with metal grommets,
a cross-tab for hanging
a pager, I suppose,
though I'd hardly know—
the only jogging I've done
is to your gate.

I'm not secure—
when I arrive
unhook me,
toss the old dog
high, across the room.

The Universal Danseuse
(night train through Quebec: December)

Queer geometries, blue isosceles lights mime pines.
Emerald bulbs chug roughshod across roofs.
Further west a random red, a lantern-flare in snow.

Your words spring onto the small screen in my hand—
Where are you?—
Someplace with lights (send)—
I don't mention neon pinks that pop the night—
'Danseuses' in the cartoon shapes of
women, always the same
woman—The Universal Danseuse,
my Anglo mind supposes. Her rosy
form above the dark doors of bars (barz?)
and who couldn't use a good stiff one
this time of year?

Someplace with lights (sent).
I'm a genius at selective geography.
I don't want you getting ideas, heaven forbid
you should picture
The Universal Danseuse, her head tipped back,
outlined in neon or even quotidian positions
like opening her presents. No, I want your mind
far from her contour-glow, miles and miles.
and miles. To you, she's lost in translation.

In the hours that follow I send you safe word-scenes:
lit crosses in villages, Home Hardwares.
How the sun at Charny rose the hue of some high-end
brand of pink grapefruit juice sluiced with berries.
How the morning-lit snow fields are a postcard.
How this province is belle for good reason.
How I, tucked in Economy Class,
my vintage fur hat with the ear-flaps
lowered, resemble a character
in a Russian novel
or a friendly campsite bear.

Travel meditation:
On the demise of modern manners

My what a lady you are, chugging along. Almost English in ivory elbow gloves, your hat's cusped veil through which kohl-lined eyes scan the dusk-green bogs, all yellow spigot-blooms on their lily pad balconies, a kind of wild bamboo that thrives with some frequency. The same tall, jointed plants thronged in the shed shadows of your childhood; if this were a story, the creaking engine of flashback would crank over at this juncture. It is impossible not to be associative on trains. The drift of moving grass pulls hard (*O the things men have said to you*). The zither-and-cream of ferns evokes a theme park of beds, green mattresses on which you are called fascinating and complex, not, as in real life, *a boa constrictor, blanket hog, cover swine.* In Train World no one would tell a lady such things. Men's manners have flown of late, simply *vaporized.* It is impossible to stay fixed by rail, gloves or no gloves. The clock slides back a decade to when he, bundled in furred emerald sheets, read you novels under the torque and thrum of the ceiling fan. Whispered you were like a sister to him (whispered with no pathology whatsoever). *Where went the art of intimate liturgy,* of *giving* a tinker's toot, you breathe to the rusted kitchen ranges out there, to the schools with their bereft summer eyes. In the flash-forward men will reptilize you more. Count on it. Your gloves might as well be snake-skins: one wound around a glass of train-beer, the other, a biography of Keats heftier than the loftiest prayer book (*so massive a book for so brief a life*). It is impossible not to possess hindsight and strong ears on trains. That congenial rasp: Keats reading to his mother at Ponders End.

TERRY ANN CARTER

Terry Ann Carter has committed numerous "Random Acts of Poetry" across Ottawa from *Waiting for Julia* (Third Eye, 1999), *Transplanted* (Borealis, 2006), and the haiku anthology *Carpe Diem* (co-editor, Les Éditions David / Borealis, 2009); "cherry blossoms" was published in *bottle rockets*, 2009, "moon" won first place in the Basho Festival Anthology, 2005, and "endless rain" received an honourable mention in the 2009 Betty Drevniok Award.

cherry blossoms
the small birthmark
just above her lip

moon
in and out of clouds
my mother's cancer tests

endless rain
in my mother's kitchen
the snap snapping of beans

Away

My children live in far away cities
where lights in midnight towers
may be confused with stars
heaven floating down on them
their lives flying open.

Cities of markets
multimedia installations
police checking passports
holding guns. There are methods
of transportation: sky trains, subways,
water taxis, cabs. And eateries
of a hundred kinds of food
on plates like palettes
of impressionistic colour
their landlords inviting them in
to dinner.

Perhaps there is a lobby in their apartment
with art on the walls that reminds them of home
perhaps a red canoe tied to a dock
or a boy with a dog by the sea.

Perhaps one night they may be
riding a bus, overhear a word
like *cowabunga* or *bonkers*.
They will be transported back to some
family gathering maybe by the side
of the river or grandma's back yard.
They will smell the roasted chickens
on the grill, their uncles smoking dope
in denim jeans and plumes of grey
spiralling out of the barbeque.

SARAH KLASSEN

Honours for Winnipeg writer Sarah Klassen's six poetry and two story collections
include The Canadian Authors' Association Award for Poetry, High Plains Fiction
Award, the Gerald Lampert Award, and the National Magazine Award (gold) for
Poetry, as well as nominations for the Pat Lowther, McNally Robinson Book-of-the-
Year, and Margaret Laurence Awards.

Road trip

You've made good headway on the highway
when the first drops fall, followed by the deluge.
Sheets of water batter the asphalt. Wild clover,
grasses violated. Barley yellow for harvest
flattened. Water-logged. But you, you'll make it
to your destination, wind-shield wipers lashing
out. It's dark, your boots mud-caked by the time
you stumble to the door. But never mind: this
is your home. It's dry and warm. Power is on,
tea steeps while the downpour turns to hail, pellets
rattle the windows, the whole cowed world opaque.
Had you pictured homecoming differently? Sun-lit,
perhaps? Someone there to welcome you, to ask you
where the hell you've been and did you really think
you could ride through storm unharmed, unsullied,
a conqueror, alone? Well, did you? Put your feet up.
Circle the steaming mug with your cold fingers.
Forget the rain-clogged fields, the ruined harvest.
A traveller needs rest on the tedious road
to Egypt. To the new Jerusalem. Or home.

Letter and reply
for Joan McGuire

"Let me describe the island
where I'm dying. The ocean
always restless, always there.
A morning warbler I've not yet seen,
a soprano, sings from a thicket,
a melody of happiness that almost
overshadows pain. I'm new here
(not new to suffering), tired, unable
to imagine spring, a green world
blossoming. Forests are orange,
crimson. The sun
flares through morning mist,
radiates the body, spills over everything
a light that's glorious and pure
enough to die for."

"Here on the prairie, autumn's beauty
is subdued. Imagine plain brown,
modest yellow. The occasional hedge
a splash of red like recent blood.
Everything's dry, the land needs rain.
Today I'll clean the eaves for winter,
hike beside the river that in spring
overflows its boundaries. Could be
I'll see the sun set fire to the sky
before retiring. I'll unfold
your latest island letter, grateful
to know the Light you wait for in the east
(as I do in the west)
can suddenly break through,
appearing everywhere."

Time

My father, a singular man, had time on his mind,
how little there was of it, how it sped hell-bent
for glory. *Man muss die Zeit auskaufen,** he said,
grinding grain for leghorns, filling the water trough,
humming a hymn. What was he thinking when he fell
so suddenly out of time? He'd intended to haul
crated eggs to the co-op. Instead, the droning feed-mill
stopped, the leghorns fidgeted as if they knew
they must be caught, crated, hauled to slaughter.
The enterprise, its hour come, shut down.
The day of burial, a vicious prairie blizzard: Snow,
like feathers in the morning, by evening needle-sharp.
You couldn't see the hen barn from the house. All space
obliterated. Time, completely spent, stood still.

(*We must redeem time.)

Crow mother

1

Crow mother, denied the gift of song,
can neither croon nor warble her dusky
children to sleep. But never think that she

resents comparison with nightingales
or finds the rawness of her voice
disturbing. She doesn't care one whit

that poets in their quest for metaphor
belabour her black helmet, black tail
feathers, unpleasantly curved claws.

No one praises her voice. But it's her
instrument, she'll employ it any way
she can. Rouse the somnolent neighbourhood,

infuriate the squirrel vying for the crude
nest she cobbled from twigs, leaves, filched
fragments of string. How dare a wingless creature

eye her property, her sanctuary, podium
from where with all her jet-black heart she loves
to berate, raucously, the known world?

Crow mother
plummets from the heady height
    and lands content on carrion.

2

Crow mother's got her two fledglings
out on a limb, scolding, urging them on
with harsh harangue until they inch forward
terrified. Imagine your own mother making you
walk the gang plank. There's no way
but forward. The first one, flapping brand new wings,
gains lift off, drop off, clumsy landing on the pavement.
The second clings with baby talons to the branch, then,
hassled by its dark parent, takes heart, takes off
and lands pinion-borne, lucky, on grass.
The proud old bird looks down. Having done her duty,
having shown crow love, she ascends to a greater height
and like a conqueror rasps out a brassy peroration
in praise of motherhood. In praise of her
most excellent accomplishment.

3

Crow mother buzzes you in the lane. You swear
you feel the air shift, a wing tip actually rakes
the crown of your head, and here she comes
again and now you see the reason: In the weeds
an ink-black dying bird. One of her own.
A member of the flock. Sister, brother, offspring,
feathers slack as a windless sail, limp, pathetic.
Don't expect her to let you pass or let this lonely
dying go unnoticed. Outraged, defiant, she will
drive all gawkers off, undertake
one last heartbroken fly-by.

PETER GIBBON

Peter Gibbon originally hails from a small town 'called Listowel in Southwestern Ontario. He recently completed an M.A. in Canadian Studies at Carleton University in Ottawa. He has been published by little Ottawa literary magazines *In/Words*, *Bywords*, *Dusty Owl Quarterly*, *Moose & Pussy*, and *Vagina Dentata*. This is his first official trade publication.

no two people

I counted four umbrellas in garbage cans today

yours is not broad enough for two people

and we don't choose which way the rain falls, it makes these decisions

without consulting us.

so I must in turn, rub off on you, plant lyrics in your ear,

stutter in the gutter down the street,

make sure your high heels or rubber boots with polka-dots don't sink in too deep,

plug the outside of your soles with my nicotine gum, or

no two people, sometimes the sun's out when it's raining,

depends on how I feel in the morning.

there are conditions, then, I guess

is what I'm learning, but

if you are a skinny umbrella, I can be a lazy MP3 player,

together / we can make the distance shorter

ROGER BELL

Roger Bell grew up in Port Elgin, Ontario, and now lives near Georgian Bay. His sixth collection, *You Tell Me*, appeared in 2009. In 2007, 2008, and 2009, Bell used his 2000 Honda Shadow ACE motorcycle to commit "Random Acts of Poetry." He taught secondary school English for 29 years.

Only place

The only place for dying is where you are.
Just lie down in the chorus of all that is familiar:
all that time-rubbed furniture that lets you sag,
the wooden floors weathered by feet coming,
then going, the dishes your hands find even in the dark
when thirst or hunger wake you in the deepest night.

Lie down on the lawn among the flowers you have sown,
the bright ox-eyed daisies and heavy peonies
that nod their heads in time to graceful tunes
sung by winds for a thousand million years,
allow the sun to soak away that age, those many aches,
let the genial grass seep up and knead your knots.

The only place for dying is where you've always been,
here, among the now and known, here where you pertain.

I have chosen

in memory of John Norton

I have chosen today to put away
the bike for winter.
I have chosen a day of unutterable beauty,
a day I *could* have ridden,
perhaps the last such one.
I have chosen this day because what is pleasure
without abnegation,
without *what if,*
without that ache in the chest that
would squeeze out tears if you allowed it?

The chrome gleams with fresh wax.
The rims that I slid the cloth-wrapped finger tip along,
erasing a film of unravelled miles and sun-splay,
of chain grease and fatigue,
seem satisfied. The saddle is at ease.
The mirrors, sharp-eyed with vinegar,
look back and back and back at summers past.

You told me once this was the prettiest bike you'd ever seen.
I wonder what comeliness you saw
on that last day along that last Nebraska river, reaching into the west,
the possibility of adjournment not the corn-fed horizon
but a small town just beyond it crowned by stars.

You did not decide to stop
the way I have—
it was chosen for you,
a sudden season you found yourself in,
past movement and sense.
I've chosen well, John,
for late tonight the heavens will thicken myopically
and by morning a banshee wind come
keening in off the grey bay and the roads slicken

with denial. Then, no one rides.
But though left behind, dismounted by the cold, I can still
take comfort in what rests ready,
in that polished promise
of postponement.

Invitation
18 November 2001, 5 am

Blythe, wake up, the sky's on fire
the stars streak towards the dawn
come, my grown child, see the Leonids
the next time they blaze like this
I likely won't be here to share

but before you leave the safety of the house
before you
step outside into that deep well of space
here
put on these thick socks of wool from off my feet
and this winter coat (it was my own dad's, remember?)
from off my back, I've warmed them with my body
they'll keep you from the frost

there's little else in life a father can do for adult daughters
but wrap them in his love, and turn their eyes to heaven.

GRANT D. SAVAGE

Ottawa naturalist and photographer Grant D. Savage's books are *The Swan's Wings* (with Ruby Spriggs), *Their White with Them* (Lampman-Scott shortlist), and *Haiku North America* (co-ed., 2009). He publishes across North America and has won the Betty Drevniok Award; the following were shortlisted for the Tree Origami Crane contest.

Inadvertently seated
where the birdman feeds them
the madman wonders
why the ducks
don't understand

A swallowtail nectars
balanced on honeysuckle
how I clung to you
when we made love
and when we parted

Newspapers
blowing across a field
black and white
print as abstract an image
as yesterday

Spring snow unnoticed
the cardinal pair
wings spread
in their moment
of melting

Where someone drew it
in window frost
the moon and I
wear for each other
the exact same smiley face

One last smash
against his reflection
the cardinal
calling it quits
breaks into song

Trumpet lilies
in an art deco vase
I open the window
so at least their perfume
can reach the sun

I was wrong
it wasn't the north wind
but winter whistling in
on hundreds
of goldeneye wings

A-NEW

DEAN STEADMAN

Dean Steadman is a poet, a graduate student in English literature at the University of Ottawa, and an associate editor at *Arc Poetry Magazine*. He has published in several Canadian journals and online magazines. His first collection of poems, *their blue drowning*, will be published by Frog Hollow Press in December 2010.

mother's day

      morning a knit of daylight hours & dishes soaking
the kitchen the only room where still a star burst
or the garden corner when the first rays burrow
& summer an unmistakable vole
      she thinks to plant the red azaleas a gift
like memories of a time & drops a stitch unravelling
the outstretched arms of a four-year-old
storming the dandelions in the backyard
      a parachute drop of silken seed
he collapses in laughter on her lap a mindful mosaic
the skeins of wool among the jams & jellies she slips
into a morning sleep hands folded in the reeds & rushes
of her printed apron & dreams of geese in scarves
sparrows in sweaters the missing handles of teacups

d-day anniversary

      summer a purpose of land
a fragrance you wear
against your skin your mouth spring
      you dance the tall grasses
by the lakeshore the band stand
a weathered shell of peeling paint
& fill your pockets with tickets
      & big band swing
the beaches piling with corpses
the light a fragment of torn sky
      written a promise of wetlands
      the sanctuary of shoreline

Laakkuluk Williamson Bathory

An Inuk of Greenlandic and English descent, Laakkuluk lives with her husband Stephen and their children Akutaq and Igimaq in Iqaluit, Nunavut. This poem, dedicated to paniga Akutaq, aapaaga Steve, Akutaup sanajinga Madeleine and the staff at Baffin Regional Hospital, was written for International Women's Day celebrations in Iqaluit in 2008.

How Akutaq came to be

She came to be like a knot on a limb
    a beautiful swirl, a snarl, a song
        a fistful of passion on a branch reaching for sunlight.

It begins like thunder rumbling in the distance.
It is powerful as ice calving from glaciers.
Incessant as two weeks of hard rain.
What was once your sweet, swollen body
has become a single large muscle uncurling in slow fast motion.
Giving birth to a child is
    the visceral smell of animals, earth, humans
    the breath of life crossing death crossing life
    the sound of a woman's body shape-shifting
    the searing taste of incandescent pain
    the vision of the minute, the present and everything
    the feel of infinity, forever and nothing.
Here and now, all the cycles you have ever noticed
the moon, the tides, night and day
    and even the hourly radio news
        have funnelled into waves
deep ins
    deep outs
        qummut...ammut
deep gatherings
    and deep flushing.
Every hand that touches you
sends streaks of confidence to your pounding heart.
Every look into your eyes
trickles warmth into your belly like melt water beneath spring ice.

The waves build onto themselves
    turn into walls that you climb
        boulders you scale
            cliff faces you master.
Your body begins to reject any distractions from that
    single goal
        of opening and releasing.
Mind and body become separate beings
and your mind is
        weak
            compared to your body.
Timiga tassa! Stop! Your mind cries out. Let me rest!
Taamaatoqanngilaq isuma! No! Your body responds. We must press on!
Your mind can't take it anymore and leaves.
It wanders hrough specks of dust floating in the air
streams into cupboards, pulls out photos from long ago memory
and tries to pour cool, soothing ether into your toiling muscles.
Your body is relentless, taking
deep ins
    deep outs
        qummut...ammut
deep gatherings
    and deep flushing.
It expels excess burdens
    out with the food
    out with the fluid.
Out! Out! We don't need these anymore!
This child must have the world for itself.
This child must move down
                down
                    down.

Bones creak open to make room
flesh begins to split and
all...breath...now...owned by...muscle...alone...
body and mind snap back together.
Every particle of existence pours into the PUSH
Every cell in the body sucks new breath for the

PUSH
     AND PUSH
         AND PUSH
And then
    that completely unbelievable surreal thing happens
    that mundane ordinary down-to-earth thing happens
        that happens every second of every day around the world.
One body brings forth another body.
One person has become two people.
Two people in love have become three people full of love.
Hands grab this other-worldly blue creature
and lay HER! on my chest
    and we rub her and rub her and rub her.
She is still blue and hasn't said a thing yet.
She isn't breathing.
She isn't breathing.
Hands grab my baby and take her away
    they slap her, slide tubes down her nose and mouth.
    I can't see her.
My love and my friend both hold me and look me straight in the eyes.
3 more seconds…10 more seconds…
    Still nothing.
    Time has stopped.
    I need to hear my baby…
CRY! AND SHE DOES.
My life is replete.
I am lying in a pool of blood, I am torn and bruised
and we have never been happier.

So how did Akutaq come to be?
She came to be like a knot on a limb.
    A beautiful swirl, a snarl, a song.
        A fistful of passion unfurling on a branch reaching into sun.

MONIQUE CHÉNIER

Monique Chénier's poetry has appeared in *Regreen: New Canadian Ecological Poetry*, *Northern Prospects: An Anthology of Northeastern Ontario Poetry*, and the solo publication *Remembering Medusa Remembering*. She was born in Sudbury and grew up in Timmins, where she teaches high-school English.

Hecate's eyes

on a visit to Toronto
i watched Hecate sleep beneath a tree

everyone agreed it was her
no mistaking her hair her dancer's feet

if she had not been sleeping
i would have known her for her eyes

there was a time when Hecate
could nail you with those eyes

she followed me home
took a plane a taxi
came north like a Canada goose
and found me
in the mirror this morning

she smelled slightly of extinction
and stale bubblegum
whispered she'd lost the look
and the world had passed her by.

Thanks so much for coming to the launch! Enjoy!

Monique Chénier

scent of anise

i've seen children screaming in her eyes
heard them drowning a thousand ways
in her songs

he did that to my dark eyed daughter
the one i named for the scent of anise
the one he raped while she thought   *starlings*

and though she's a survivor of mudslides
i still brush sand from her eyes
wipe monsters from her mouth

watch as she walks carefully
whenever it rains
listen as she sings of black birds
whenever it pours.

MARY LEE BRAGG

Mary Lee Bragg grew up in Calgary, and has lived in Ottawa since 1981. Most of her career in the federal public service involved official languages; her novel *Shooting Angels* is set during the 1995 Quebec Referendum. Her poetry appeared in the anthology *Oblique Strokes*.

This Girl

I

June disappeared in September
of our grade ten year—
one day there,
       the next a vacant desk.

In the busy narrative of our lives
her absence was a footnote.
We did not ask
      where she had gone.

Decades later she finds me,
we meet for lunch and I finally ask
what happened.
      Where did you go?

"Do you remember my mother?"
I remember coolness, a cloud of disapproval
when we played records and danced
      around the bedroom they shared.

"I came home from school one day," says June,
"and there was a woman in our living room.
My mother said:

      This girl is strong—
      this girl has good teeth—
      don't take lip from this girl."

II

The strange woman wanted a nanny,
found a child in need and took her home.

I never went back, June says. They're my family now.
We're all going to Mexico next week for a cruise.

Lamb and blue cheese cool on my plate
while my universe readjusts.

I remember my mother that year—
unfeeling woman—she made me wear

hand-knit sweaters, packed fruit in my lunches,
trashed my cigarettes.

Her mouth full of pins, she bent where I stood
on a chair to mark a hem.

"Mo-om! It's too loooong!"
She pulled the pins, sighed.

"Half an inch. I'll go up half an inch and not
one bit more.

That's good wool flannel
and I won't cut it."

CLAUDIA COUTU RADMORE

Claudia Coutu Radmore's new book is *Arctic Twilight* (Blue Butterfly Books, 2010). These poems describe her pet Green-Naped Rainbow Lorikeet—an Australasian parrot smaller than a crow. "wild" was in the series that won the 2009 CAA (Ottawa) award; "sacrament" was shortlisted for the 2009 Tree Origami Crane contest.

wild

calm on my knee
this female psittacine...
two of her toes pointing forward
two backwards

her four-chambered heart beats slowly
blue cheek and chin feathers fall
smooth from their delicate hooks

descended from theropod and archaeopteryx
related to crocodile
with three eyelids
a retina twice as thick as mine
an additional colour channel
that picks up the ultraviolet
to near ultraviolet range

she twists her head backwards
to access her uropygial gland
begins to preen
her three thousand feathers
rump thumb and wingpit keratin
slides through her beak

alula bastard wings
and fused pygostyle
let her whip around room
or forest

though monogamous
bonded to me and serene
there is danger in her hooked
downcurved upper mandible
smaller upcurved lower mandible

last week
just for a moment
i forgot her great need
for my full attention
forgot her lightning quick responses
when she doesn't have it

she took a chunk out of my face
just above where
my operculum would be
if i were the wild feathered love partner
she would prefer

sacrament

if she is on my knee
and i close my eyes
she remains still for a few moments
considering
i feel her feet tentative on my thigh
then she walks up to my folded hands
      slow as a cloistered nun in meditation
lays the side of her beak against my skin
it is warm
      its touch soft as the breath of a holy ghost
bristled hairs above her beak
bless my knuckle like gentle oiled thumb
      of priest at font

should this be the day
my eyes do not open again
she will sit there doing that
      performing the rite
      in silent vigil

DEE HOBSBAWN-SMITH

dee Hobsbawn-Smith, an award-winning gastronomic writer, chef, and educator, recently moved to a small farm in Saskatchewan after 27 years in Calgary. She shortlisted for the *Malahat Review's* 2009 Far Horizons Short Fiction award and for the 2010 Far Horizons Poetry award. Her poetry has appeared in *Room*, *Other Voices*, and *The Antigonish Review*, among others.

Contemplating breast surgery
for Judith

The naming of a breast
is simple
to cooks, and surgeons, the recipe's
bland print—

one breast, boneless—

drooping soft from the breastbone,
no muscles or tendons or ribcage bars to protect it
from the call of hunger,
eager cutting hands.

One breast or half?
How much is enough?

French cooks, tired of wrestling with such questions,
name pairs or parts or singles
together in submission beneath the knife,
simplify:

      magret.

But what is good for cooks
is soul-less. In the flesh, I prefer uncut
feminine names, round with open vowels and
sweet sibilant consonants, name them in polite company.

Meet my breasts:
Francesca. Consuela.

Amanda Earl

Ottawa poet Amanda Earl was shortlisted for the 2009 Robert Kroetsch Award for Innovative Poetry. Recent work appears in *Rogue Stimulus: The Stephen Harper Holiday Anthology* (Mansfield, 2010), *this is visual poetry* (chapbookpublisher, 2010), *Welcome to Earth: Poem for Alien(s)* (BookThug, 2008), and *Eleanor and The Sad Phoenician's Other Woman* (above/ground, 2007/2008). (www.amandaearl.com)

rain

we are voyeurs in love with weather.
i make appointments with you to watch the sky open up.

yesterday i waited alone for a bus and threw my broken umbrella in the
trash.
let myself be thoroughly drenched.

on these summer days when the sky is blue and silent, oh how i miss the
rain.
have noticed my heartbeat can't tell the difference between you and a down-
pour.

the weather this year

you have been raining, finally raining
there is more, more water, more rain

you wade into it, there's no question
that you thirst, the quenching drops persist,

are intermittent then drowning, how you wish: submerged
streetlamps reflect on the ripples of flooded sidewalks

this shade of blue exists only in renaissance paintings and rainy nights
you have such ocean cravings, all of this spilling down

down into storm pipes, for now you are in between downpours
but you know the rain will come again, hard again

next time you'll throw everything away
this umbrella and anything that shields

CAMERON ANSTEE

Cameron Anstee lives in Ottawa, Ontario, where he runs Apt. 9 Press (apt9press.ca) and works at Octopus Books. Recent chapbooks include *Frank St.* (above/ground, 2010) and *Water Upsets Stone* (The Emergency Response Unit, 2009), from which "First Law" is an excerpt.

First Law

i. A body maintains its state of rest or motion in a straight line unless acted on by an external force.

—Isaac Newton, *Three Laws of Motion*

we have been standing this whole time

branches refuse leaves
carry less weight in to winter

but lengthen in ground to upset foundations
poured for brick, how water upsets stone

I am not sure where to locate the tree
or when

/

in the ice storm a tree hung
its glass to the tops of our cars

I don't remember the trees before '98
the storm's linger knows no thing of origin

my whole life then
half my life now

/

history impressing

shovel down to the drive &
bury the earlier work

the plough cutting away in sheets
a larger mountain in cross-section

baring strata
small crumbling in the air

/

snow evenly   sheered

                              the open
refusing gravity

& tiny seasons where grass continues

bricks contracting toward their empty spaces

/

surface tension above
the glass lip

a fluid coherence
of small matter

pulling inward & swollen

/

body is energy is body

want no distinctions
no thing between skin

*the energy produced
by the movements of a substance's*

atoms

it is cold out
but our room is very warm

it is cold out
our room is warm

/

you stand
all the air moves

/

resolve the bend of light
into spectrums

play gravity with snow
play water in eaves

the sun our only gauge of size
& more size

gravitational potential
      & falling & falling

kinesis

my mass
& your mass

/

I examine your body, & then mine
a construction other than clear angles

only movements
white where skin reaches, & removes

we met in a long kiss
& newly arranged our weight

/

where the energy is
before falling

I remember where we were standing .

Jeremy Hanson-Finger

Jeremy Hanson-Finger is one of the founding editors of *the Moose & Pussy*, Ottawa's only literary erotica magazine.

Passover

They hid in the swamp
and they were saved.

2. Prologue

They'd killed Tsar Alexander, just like they'd killed the Son of Man. Or at least, that's what the men with the dogs said. They panted it out in thick clouds that Great-Grandmother could see rise above the pines while she crouched in the swamp for the first time, water just warm enough to be fluid, trying not so much to stop shivering as just to match her muscles' jumping to the movement of the wind-shook rushes.

3. 1919

In 1919's swamp, the men and dogs came thirty times.

—Twelve times it was the chief of the military who sent them.

—Five times it was the White Army.

—Eight times it was the Green Armies.

—Twice it was the Red Army, but those visits weren't official, the rifle snouts wavering ten feet away nothing but spectres of rifle snouts because the men were on their own time.

Now it was summer and the water was warmer but mosquitoes sunk
needles into her and she couldn't swat them, instead dripped waterfalls
of blood down her legs, a scale model of the Tsar's red rapids flowing into
the Catherine Canal thirty years before, praying as she had been
encouraged to do and as her parents and brothers and sisters were doing,
all quietly and with shallow breaths, below the amplitude of the wind's
sighs.

4. 2009

In another now,
this now that you and I are in,
when we lie here and the sheet is soaked through
            between your legs
and it's not even deep enough
for it to pool and breed mosquitoes overnight,
and you roll over and reach for a towel to lay over it so
            we can sleep like abstract ideas that don't leak fluids
            all over each other,
I kind of want you to leave it,
don't mind the clamminess of evaporation on my skin because
I feel like I owe something to Great-Grandmother
and her family back in Kiev
in 1919—

1. Conclusion

NOTES

"Executive Suite," pp. 78-83.
This suite of poems was written in the 1980s during the period when Erín Moure and Bronwen Wallace (1945-1989) were exchanging letters on feminist poetics, narrative, and language theory.

"Chaos poem" and "Life mask," pp. 110 and 112.
Margaret Atwood contributed these two poems to the preview issue of *Branching Out*, Canada's first national feminist and arts magazine, which I and a group of collaborators founded in Edmonton in 1973. Her agreement to have them appear for the second time in *Pith & Wry* is significant to Canadian literature, since "Life mask" has been published to date only in *Branching Out*, and "Chaos poem," published in *You Are* Happy (1974), is otherwise uncollected.

CREDITS

The poems on the following pages previously appeared in *Sugar Mule* #33 (sugarmule.com): 14-23, 28-35, 38-49, 54-68, 73-77, 86-89, 94-102, 106-07, 113-14, 117-21, 126, 128-34, 140-44, 146-51. At the time, almost all the poems were otherwise unpublished. During the preparation of *Pith & Wry*, many have since been slightly revised or have appeared in authors' collections. All poems are published with permission of the copyright holders. Credits for poems generally appear with the poems, with the following exceptions:

"The Swallowing," p. 90
This poem is one of a series published in *All the Clubs from Holyrood to Brigus*," the exhibition catalogue for a show by photographer Scott Walden, Grenfell College Art Gallery in November 2009.

"Vertical Panel," p. 92
"This cento is one of a much larger collection," writes Mary Dalton. "It happens that this one is drawn from American poets; many others draw on Canadians, as well as poets from other countries." Each line of the cento consists of the second line of the following poems:

1. Stephen Dunn, "Connubial"
2. Bruce McKinnon, "The Bees"
3. Louise Glück, "The Drowned Children"
4. Louise Glück, "Palais des Arts"

5. Marvin Bell, "Drawn by Stones, by Earth, by Things that Have Been in the Fire".
6. Marvin Bell, "The Self and the Mulberry"
7. James Dickey, "The Strength of Fields"
8. J. V. Cunningham, "To My Wife"

9. Randall Jarrell, "Eighth Air Force"
10. John Hollander, "Mad Potter"
11. Charles Wright, "Clear Night"
12. Sandra McPherson, "The Microscope in Winter"

13. Howard Nemerov, "Learning the Trees"
14. Jean Garrigue, "Cracked Looking-Glass"
15. William Meredith, "Country Stars"
16. Jorie Graham, "Orpheus and Eurydice"

17. Richard Hugo, "Degrees of Gray in Philipsburg"
18. Mark Strand, "The Story of Our Lives"
19. Howard Moss, "Rules of Sleep"
20. Irving Feldman, "Simple Outlines, Human Shapes"

21. John Berryman, "The Moon and the Night and the Men"
22. Amy Clampitt, "Medusa"
23. Edward Hirsch, "Fast Break"
24. Anne Sexton, "The Starry Night"

25. Theodore Roethke, "The Shape of the Fire"
26. Elizabeth Bishop, "Poem"
27. John Hollander, "The Night Mirror"
28. John Ashbery, "Glazunoviana"

INDEX OF POETS, PLACES, FIRST LINES